Benchmark Assessments
Teacher Edition
Grade 4

Senior Author
Dr. Roger C. Farr

Chancellor's Professor Emeritus,
Indiana University, Bloomington

Harcourt School Publishers

www.harcourtschool.com

Copyright © by Harcourt, Inc.

All rights reserved. No part of this publication may be reproduced or transmitted in any form or by any means, electronic or mechanical, including photocopy, recording, or any information storage and retrieval system, without permission in writing from the publisher.

Permission is hereby granted to individuals using the corresponding student's textbook or kit as the major vehicle for regular classroom instruction to photocopy Fluency forms from this publication in classroom quantities for instructional use and not for resale. Requests for information on other matters regarding duplication of this work should be addressed to School Permissions and Copyrights, Harcourt, Inc., 6277 Sea Harbor Drive, Orlando, Florida 32887-6777. Fax: 407-345-2418.

HARCOURT and the Harcourt Logo are trademarks of Harcourt, Inc., registered in the United States of America and/or other jurisdictions.

Printed in the United States of America

ISBN 10   0-15-358762-8   ISBN 13   978-0-15-358762-7

1 2 3 4 5 6 7 8 9 10   073   16 15 14 13 12 11 10 09 08 07

**Property of
Upper Iowa University
Waterloo Curriculum Lab**

> If you have received these materials as examination copies free of charge, Harcourt School Publishers retains title to the materials and they may not be resold. Resale of examination copies is strictly prohibited and is illegal.

> Possession of this publication in print format does not entitle users to convert this publication, or any portion of it, into electronic format.

Contents

Developing the *Benchmark Assessments*... T3

Overview T5

Administering the Oral Reading Fluency Tests T7

Item Analyses T14

Scoring Responses to Open-Ended Items T23

Scoring Responses to Writing Prompts T27

Assessment Booklets

    Beginning-of-Year Test, Mid-Year Test, End-of-Year Test

Developing the *Benchmark Assessments*

From *StoryTown* Senior Author

Dr. Roger C. Farr

"Every teacher's primary concern is helping students learn. . . . Teachers are primarily interested in the kind of information that will support the daily instructional decisions they need to make."

Validity and Reliability

The *Benchmark Assessments* are comprised of Beginning-of-Year, Mid-Year, and End-of-Year tests that closely parallel national and state reading assessments. Additionally, program authors and editors conducted a careful alignment of the assessments to states' Reading and Language Arts standards. The result is a set of tests that are closely linked to both national and state language arts standards, assuring their content validity.

The empirical validity of the tests was assured through a tryout that included over 14,000 students at grades 1 to 6 in school districts throughout the United States. Eight different states covering major geographic areas of the country and representing diverse demographics were included in the tryout, as were over 650 classrooms. The schools were located in large cities, small cities, suburbs of both medium and large cities, and rural areas. The socioeconomic population of the schools closely paralleled that of the entire population of the United States. The tryout data affirmed an overarching intent of the test development, which was an increase in the difficulty of the tests from grade to grade as well as across the Beginning-of-Year, Mid-Year, and End-of-Year tests at each grade.

Field-Test Design

All assessments were administered by regular classroom teachers and returned to Indiana University for scoring and analysis. Standardized directions were provided for each teacher. Suggested test sittings and approximate testing times were provided; however, teachers were encouraged to allow sufficient time for all students to complete the assessments.

Although each reading selection and set of comprehension questions was targeted for a particular grade-level, the passages and items were often field-tested one grade above and one grade below the targeted level to gain a better estimate of item difficulty for students at various grade levels.

The item analysis data included the number and percent of students choosing each response option or omitting the item. Point-biserial item discrimination indices were also calculated for each item by grade level. These item-level statistics formed the primary sets of data used to select the final passages and items and to make appropriate item revisions.

Each participating teacher also completed a questionnaire, indicating the appropriateness of the passages and items, the interest level of the materials, and the clarity of the directions.

Based on the field-test data, the *Benchmark Assessments* were finalized for *StoryTown.*

Developing the *Benchmark Assessments*

Overview

Use the *Benchmark Assessments* to assess students' mastery of the skills taught in the program. The Beginning-of-Year test will tell you what skill areas students may need help in during the upcoming year. The Mid-Year and End-of-Year tests will tell you what skill areas students are mastering and what areas they need additional support in. The Mid-Year and End-of-Year tests are summative; they assess what has been taught in the program up to the point of administration. The *Benchmark Assessments* can be administered over multiple sessions. Use the results of the tests to modify instruction and meet students' individual learning needs. The *Benchmark Assessments* assess reading comprehension, word analysis and vocabulary, writing strategies and conventions, writing to a prompt, and oral reading fluency.

About the Test Sections

Reading Comprehension
This section assesses comprehension of grade-level text. Each multiple-choice item is worth one point. Each short written response item is worth two points, and each extended written response item is worth four points. See page T23 for the scoring rubric and sample top-scoring responses.

Vocabulary and Word Analysis
This section assesses students' understanding of Robust Vocabulary taught in the program and their word analysis skills.

Writing Strategies and Conventions
This multiple-choice section assesses students' understanding of writing strategies and grammar skills.

Writing to a Prompt
This section asks students to respond to a writing prompt. See page T27 for directions for scoring and model responses.

Oral Reading Fluency
Assessing oral reading fluency will help you determine how well a student can apply decoding skills and recognize words quickly. Both narrative and expository passages are provided. The readability has been controlled so that the text is on grade level for students. See page T7 for directions and recording forms.

Scoring and Interpreting the *Benchmark Assessments*

The *Benchmark Assessments* can be scored using the Item Analyses. Follow these steps:
1. Turn to the appropriate Item Analysis on pages T14–T22. (Please see page T7 for scoring and interpreting the Oral Reading Fluency section.)
2. Compare the student's responses, item by item, to the Item Analysis and put a check mark next to each item that is correctly answered. For scoring the open-ended items, please see page T23. For scoring the Writing to a Prompt section, please see page T27.
3. Count the number of correct responses for each test section and write this number on the "Student Score" line on the Performance Summary.
4. Compare the student's total scores for each section to the performance levels provided below the "Student Score" section.

A student who scores at or above the Basic level for each test section is considered competent in that skill area and is probably ready to move forward without additional practice, except for ongoing maintenance.

A student who does not reach the Basic level probably needs additional instruction and/or practice in that particular skill area. Examine the student's scores for each test section and decide whether you should reteach a particular skill, or move forward to the next theme.

Please note: the performance levels are only provided as a guideline for interpreting a student's performance. A *Benchmark Assessment* is just one observation of a student's reading and writing behavior. It should be combined with other evidence of a student's progress, such as the teacher's daily observations, student's work samples, and individual conferences. The sum of all this information is more valid and reliable than any single piece of information.

Overview

Administering the Oral Reading Fluency Tests

To administer the fluency assessment, use the Oral Reading Fluency Recording Forms and a stopwatch or second hand. Student copies of the passages are provided with each *Benchmark Assessment*. All of the passages are "fresh reads" that students have not read before.

Directions for Administering

1. Explain the task to the student. Tell the student that you want to see how well he or she can read aloud. Inform the student that you will follow along as he or she reads, taking notes. The student may ask about being timed. Encourage him or her to read at his or her "normal" pace. You don't want the student to speed up and read artificially fast because of the timing.
2. Have the student begin. Time a one-minute interval.
3. As the student reads, record reading errors unobtrusively on the Recording Form. Mark mispronunciations, substitutions, omissions of a sound or word, and other errors. *Do not count repetitions or self-corrections as reading errors.*
4. When the time reaches the one-minute mark, place a slash mark on the Oral Reading Fluency Recording Form after the last word the student reads. Tell the student to stop reading.

Computing the Fluency Score

1. Total the number of words read by the student in one minute. The row numbers in the right margin will help you determine the number.
2. Count the number of reading errors the student made.
3. Subtract the number of reading errors made from the total number of words read correctly. This is the student's oral reading fluency score. Write the words correctly read per minute (WCPM) on the Performance Summary.

Interpreting the Fluency Score

The norms below are based on a study conducted by Hasbrouck and Tindal (2006) in which they established fluency norms for Grades 1 through 8. Look at the WCPM norms below, finding the column that corresponds most closely to the time of year the test was given, and compare the student's score to the norms. Students reading below the 50th percentile may require additional instruction to improve oral reading fluency.

Grade 4 Oral Reading Fluency Norms			
Percentile	**Fall**	**Winter**	**Spring**
25th	68	87	98
50th	94	112	123
75th	119	139	152

Source: Hasbrouck, Jan, and Gerald A. Tindal. 2006. Oral reading fluency norms: A valuable assessment tool for reading teachers. *Reading Teacher* 59 (April), no. 7: 636-644.

Name _____

Benchmark Assessment

Beginning-of-Year

Oral Reading Fluency

Have you ever seen a picture of earthworms in a garden? Or,	12
have you seen one near the edge of a sidewalk? They seem so	25
ordinary we hardly think they are worth noticing. However,	34
there are about 3,000 different kinds of these worms. Although	44
we know quite a bit about them, they can still amaze us.	56
Earthworms belong to a group of worms whose bodies are	66
divided into sections. These sections work together to allow	75
the worm to travel. When you see an earthworm crawling, pay	86
attention to how it moves.	91
Another special detail about the worm is that it is hard to tell	104
where its head is. You can't tell by looking in its eyes. That is	118
because this worm does not have eyes like people do. The worm	130
can just sense light and dark. The end with the mouth is more	143
pointed than the other end, and that is how you can tell where	156
the head is.	159
An earthworm's skin must stay wet in order for it to live. If	172
its skin dries out, the worm dies. Therefore, worms prefer damp	183
places, like soil. A worm does not breathe the way you do. It	196
takes in oxygen through its skin.	202
Perhaps the earthworm is not quite so common after all.	212

Oral Reading Fluency Recording Forms

Harcourt • Grade 4

Name _____

Benchmark Assessment

Beginning-of-Year

Lynn swam smoothly between the ocean waves. As the	9
water rolled across her shiny, gray back, she glanced over at her	21
mother swimming with a group of her friends a short distance	32
away. Swiftly, pretending she was an arrow, she plunged straight	42
down into the waves, swimming very rapidly. Next she pushed	52
her powerful body straight up into the sky as high as she could.	65
She broke the surface next to her mother with an enormous	76
splash. Her mother splashed her back with a mighty wave of her	88
flipper.	89
They played in the salty water until a strange sight on the	101
beach caught Lynn's attention. She stopped swimming and	109
stared at two strange, upright creatures who were facing her	119
and pointing. She wondered what they were, and her mother	129
explained to her that those were two human beings. Lynn could	140
see the people waving at her, so she waved back with her great,	153
flexible tail. Mother then suggested to Lynn that they begin the	164
search for lunch. Lynn swam in place beside her mother. She	175
realized that no life could be more wonderful than hers—life as	187
a bottlenose dolphin.	190

Oral Reading Fluency
Recording Forms

Name _____

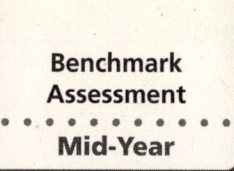

Oral Reading Fluency

    Sam's mother was concerned because Sam would not eat his   10
vegetables. He said that he didn't like how they tasted. Mom   21
repeatedly told him that he had to eat his vegetables to grow up   34
a strong and healthy individual. But Sam stubbornly refused.   43

    Margaret, Sam's sister, attempted to help by encouraging   51
Sam to eat vegetables, saying that they really taste delicious.   61
Margaret's favorite vegetable is corn. She liked her corn   70
with peppers and a pat of butter. But Sam wouldn't touch it.   82
Margaret chewed on a fresh carrot, but Sam chose not to join   94
her in chomping on one.   99

    Mom and Margaret were stumped and could not decide   108
what to do, but then Margaret had an idea. She winked at   120
her mother. Mom smiled and nodded and they went into the   131
kitchen, while Sam went outdoors to play.   138

    Soon Sam came into the kitchen, sniffing the air. Something   148
really smelled good! Freshly baked, piping hot cookies were   157
sitting on the kitchen table. Sam ate three cookies and said they   169
were the best he had ever tasted. They were very flavorful and   181
very chewy. Mom and Margaret laughed, which surprised Sam,   190
so he asked what the joke was.   197

    Mom told him the cookies were made with lots of   207
carrots, which made the cookies both chewy and sweet. Sam   217
reconsidered his opinion about vegetables and began to try   226
them at least one at every meal.   233

**Oral Reading Fluency
Recording Forms**
Harcourt • Grade 4

Name _____

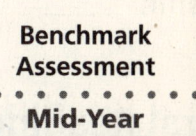

Some people think of bats as fearsome, but instead of being	11
harmful, bats are quite interesting and helpful.	18
One surprising fact about bats is that they are the only	29
mammals that truly fly. There are almost 1,000 different kinds	39
of bats, and they all fly.	45
Bats have an unusual skill when it comes to finding their	56
way around. Many kinds of bats don't see well. But they use	68
their hearing in a very special way. They make a high-pitched	80
sound and listen to its echo as it bounces off objects. Although	92
a few kinds of bats do see and smell well, most kinds of bats use	107
this unusual method of "seeing" as they fly and hunt.	117
Insects, not people, are the ones who should be scared	127
of bats. One small brown bat can catch and eat up to 600	140
mosquitoes in a single hour. That's a skill you might be thankful	152
for if you've ever had a mosquito bite. Bats also fertilize plants	164
as they fly from one plant to the other, and they scatter plant	177
seeds. Both of these actions help new plants to grow.	187
Each of us decides whether or not to be afraid of bats. The	200
more you know about bats, the more you realize how helpful	211
they are.	213

Name _____

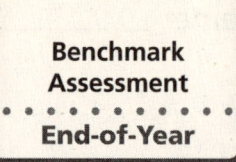

Benchmark Assessment
End-of-Year

Oral Reading Fluency

Sometimes ordinary creatures can turn out to be rather	9
unusual. Spiders, for example, can be interesting to study,	18
though we might consider them to be relatively common.	27
Spiders belong to a group of creatures that have four pairs of	39
legs—eight legs in all. That makes them different from insects,	50
which have three pairs of legs—six legs. This difference is an	62
important way to tell whether a little crawling creature is a	73
spider. The body of a spider has two parts, so if you see only one	88
body part or you see three body parts, you're not looking at a	101
spider.	102
Spiders have a special skill that is well-known: they produce	113
a fine, very strong silk from glands at the rear of their bodies.	126
This silk has several uses. Probably the one you are most	137
familiar with is the spider web that you might notice on a bush,	150
or in a quiet, unused corner of a room. Spiders also use the silk	164
to line burrows and nests. Spiders also wrap their eggs in the	176
fiber. Finally, spiders make little parachutes with it so they can	187
float through the air to new places.	194
Observe those spiders crawling and spinning around us every	203
day. They're worth examining!	207

Name _____

Benchmark Assessment

End-of-Year

Dear Thomas,

    You're in for a surprise when you come to visit next month! Do you remember how I always hated to rake the lawn and weed the vegetable garden? Whenever Dad told me to get busy on the jobs, I would tell him that I would do them later. Of course, you also remember that "later" never arrived. Then I would be reminded, and I would find another excuse. The result was always all of us getting "irritated," you might say.

    Anyhow, I was treated to a moral lesson in a BIG way. I delayed doing a school project until the last minute, actually until too late. When I could not complete it on time, I begged my dad to talk to my teacher about an extension of the deadline. Of course, my dad would not do any such thing. He told me he loved me, but that it was very important that I finish my jobs on time. He said that I need *self-discipline*.

    Well, you will find me so full of self-discipline when you get here that I hope you'll still recognize me! I know mowing the lawn and weeding the garden are my jobs, so I just do them. No discussion necessary. Dad and Mom say I've grown up. Of course, I'm proud to help keep the estate's lawn green. See you soon.

                        Your friend,
                         Emilio

Dear Thomas,	2
You're in for a surprise when you come to visit next month!	14
Do you remember how I always hated to rake the lawn and	26
weed the vegetable garden? Whenever Dad told me to get busy	37
on the jobs, I would tell him that I would do them later. Of	51
course, you also remember that "later" never arrived. Then I	61
would be reminded, and I would find another excuse. The result	72
was always all of us getting "irritated," you might say.	82
Anyhow, I was treated to a moral lesson in a BIG way. I	95
delayed doing a school project until the last minute, actually	105
until too late. When I could not complete it on time, I begged	118
my dad to talk to my teacher about an extension of the	130
deadline. Of course, my dad would not do any such thing.	141
He told me he loved me, but that it was very important that I	155
finish my jobs on time. He said that I need self-discipline.	166
Well, you will find me so full of self-discipline when you get	178
here that I hope you'll still recognize me! I know mowing the	190
lawn and weeding the garden are my jobs, so I just do them.	203
No discussion necessary. Dad and Mom say I've grown up. Of	214
course, I'm proud to help keep the estate's lawn green. See you	226
soon.	227
Your friend,	229
Emilio	230

Oral Reading Fluency
Recording Forms

Item Analysis: Beginning-of-Year

Reading Comprehension

Item	Correct Answer	Skill	Cognitive Complexity*	Webb's Depth of Knowledge**
1	C	Character, Setting, and Plot	High	Level 3
2	G	Use Context Clues	Moderate	Level 2
3	B	Character, Setting, and Plot	Moderate	Level 2
4	F	Character, Setting, and Plot	Moderate	Level 2
5	A	Predict Outcomes	High	Level 3
6	*	Author's Purpose and Perspective	High	Level 3
* See page T23 for the scoring rubric and model top-scoring responses.				
7	I	Synonyms and Antonyms	Moderate	Level 2
8	A	Author's Purpose and Perspective	Moderate	Level 2
9	I	Compare and Contrast	High	Level 3
10	C	Use Context Clues	Moderate	Level 2
11	G	Main Idea and Details	Moderate	Level 2
12	*	Main Idea and Details	Moderate	Level 2
* See page T23 for the scoring rubric and model top-scoring responses.				
13	B	Character, Setting, and Plot	Low	Level 1
14	G	Character, Setting, and Plot	Low	Level 1
15	A	Predict Outcomes	Moderate	Level 2
16	G	Character, Setting, and Plot	Moderate	Level 2
17	D	Theme	Moderate	Level 2
18	*	Character, Setting, and Plot	High	Level 3
* See page T23 for the scoring rubric and model top-scoring responses.				
19	F	Compare and Contrast	High	Level 3
20	C	Locate Information	Moderate	Level 2
21	F	Main Idea and Details	Low	Level 1
22	B	Fact and Opinion	Moderate	Level 2
23	F	Make Inferences	High	Level 3
24	D	Sequence: Story Events	Low	Level 1
25	F	Main Idea and Details	Low	Level 1
26	D	Use Context Clues	Moderate	Level 2
27	F	Make Inferences	Moderate	Level 2
28	C	Character, Setting, and Plot	Moderate	Level 2
29	F	Character, Setting, and Plot	Moderate	Level 2
30	D	Main Idea and Details	Low	Level 1
31	G	Text Structure: Sequence	Low	Level 1
32	D	Use Context Clues	Moderate	Level 2
33	H	Locate Information	High	Level 3
34	C	Locate Information	Low	Level 1
35	H	Locate Information	Low	Level 1

Item Analysis: Beginning-of-Year

Vocabulary and Word Analysis				
Item	Correct Answer	Skill	Cognitive Complexity	Webb's Depth of Knowledge
36	A	Robust Vocabulary	Moderate	Level 2
37	G	Robust Vocabulary	Moderate	Level 2
38	B	Robust Vocabulary	Moderate	Level 2
39	F	Robust Vocabulary	Moderate	Level 2
40	C	Robust Vocabulary	Moderate	Level 2
41	H	Robust Vocabulary	Moderate	Level 2
42	B	Robust Vocabulary	Moderate	Level 2
43	H	Robust Vocabulary	Moderate	Level 2
44	B	Robust Vocabulary	Moderate	Level 2
45	F	Robust Vocabulary	Moderate	Level 2
46	C	Prefixes, Suffixes, and Roots	Moderate	Level 2
47	I	Prefixes, Suffixes, and Roots	Moderate	Level 2
48	A	Prefixes, Suffixes, and Roots	Moderate	Level 2
49	H	Prefixes, Suffixes, and Roots	Moderate	Level 2
50	D	Prefixes, Suffixes, and Roots	Moderate	Level 2
51	F	Use Context Clues	Moderate	Level 2
52	D	Use Context Clues	Moderate	Level 2
53	H	Synonyms and Antonyms	Moderate	Level 2
54	B	Synonyms and Antonyms	Moderate	Level 2
55	G	Synonyms and Antonyms	Moderate	Level 2
Writing Strategies and Conventions				
56	B	Writing Strategies	Moderate	Level 2
57	G	Writing Strategies	Moderate	Level 2
58	C	Writing Strategies	Moderate	Level 2
59	G	Writing Strategies	Moderate	Level 2
60	A	Writing Strategies	Moderate	Level 2
61	F	Writing Strategies	Moderate	Level 2
62	C	Writing Strategies	Moderate	Level 2
63	G	Writing Strategies	Moderate	Level 2
64	C	Writing Strategies	Moderate	Level 2
65	F	Writing Strategies	Moderate	Level 2
66	A	Adverbs	Moderate	Level 2
67	F	Past and Future Tenses	Moderate	Level 2
68	B	Contractions and Possessive Pronouns	Moderate	Level 2
69	F	Words with Prefixes: *re-, un-, non-*	Moderate	Level 2
70	C	Comparing with Adjectives	Moderate	Level 2
71	F	Present Tense: Subject/Verb Agreement	Moderate	Level 2
72	B	Common and Proper Nouns	Moderate	Level 2
73	F	Punctuation Round-up	Moderate	Level 2
74	B	Subjects and Predicates	Moderate	Level 2
75	G	Subjects and Predicates	Moderate	Level 2
76	D	Words with Prefixes: *re-, un-, non-*	Moderate	Level 2

Item Analysis: Beginning-of-Year

Writing Strategies and Conventions					
Item	Correct Answer	Skill	Cognitive Complexity	Webb's Depth of Knowledge
77	F	Words with Consonant –le	Moderate	Level 2
78	B	Words with Ending /ər/	Moderate	Level 2
79	G	Words with Suffixes: -ant, -ent, -eer, -ist, -ian	Moderate	Level 2
80	D	Word Parts in-, out-, down-, up-	Moderate	Level 2
Writing to a Prompt				
See page T25 for scoring rubric and model responses.				
Oral Reading Fluency				
See page T7 for Oral Reading Fluency Norms.				

Item Analysis: Beginning-of-Year

Item Analysis: Mid-Year

		Reading Comprehension		
Item	Correct Answer	Skill	Cognitive Complexity	Webb's Depth of Knowledge
1	A	Prefixes, Suffixes, and Roots	Moderate	Level 2
2	H	Make Inferences	Moderate	Level 2
3	B	Text Structure: Cause and Effect	Low	Level 1
4	H	Text Structure: Sequence	Low	Level 1
5	C	Figurative Language	Moderate	Level 2
6	F	Compare and Contrast	Moderate	Level 2
7	A	Character, Setting, and Plot	Low	Level 1
8	I	Use Context Clues	Low	Level 1
9	D	Character, Setting, and Plot	Moderate	Level 2
10	H	Plot: Conflict and Resolution	Moderate	Level 2
11	C	Character, Setting, and Plot	Low	Level 1
12	I	Theme	Moderate	Level 2
13	*	Plot: Conflict and Resolution	Moderate	Level 2
		* See page T23 for the scoring rubric and model top-scoring responses.		
14	B	Main Idea and Details	High	Level 3
15	I	Use Context Clues	Moderate	Level 2
16	B	Main Idea and Details	Low	Level 1
17	H	Figurative Language	Moderate	Level 2
18	A	Compare and Contrast	Moderate	Level 2
19	*	Text Structure: Cause and Effect	High	Level 3
		* See page T23 for the scoring rubric and model top-scoring responses.		
20	H	Synonyms and Antonyms	High	Level 3
21	C	Plot: Conflict and Resolution	Moderate	Level 2
22	F	Sequence: Story Events	Low	Level 1
23	C	Text Structure: Cause and Effect	Moderate	Level 2
24	G	Compare and Contrast	High	Level 3
25	A	Main Idea and Details	Low	Level 1
26	H	Character's Traits and Motivations	Moderate	Level 2
27	B	Plot: Conflict and Resolution	Low	Level 1
28	F	Fact and Opinion	Low	Level 1
29	B	Make Inferences	High	Level 3
30	F	Locate Information	Low	Level 1
31	C	Use Context Clues	Moderate	Level 2
32	G	Predict Outcomes	High	Level 3
33	C	Locate Information	Low	Level 1
34	I	Locate Information	Moderate	Level 2
35	*	Author's Purpose and Perspective	Moderate	Level 2
		* See page T23 for the scoring rubric and model top-scoring responses.		

Item Analysis: Mid-Year

Vocabulary and Word Analysis				
Item	Correct Answer	Skill	Cognitive Complexity	Webb's Depth of Knowledge
36	D	Robust Vocabulary	Moderate	Level 2
37	H	Robust Vocabulary	Moderate	Level 2
38	A	Robust Vocabulary	Moderate	Level 2
39	I	Robust Vocabulary	Moderate	Level 2
40	B	Robust Vocabulary	Moderate	Level 2
41	F	Robust Vocabulary	Moderate	Level 2
42	D	Robust Vocabulary	Moderate	Level 2
43	H	Robust Vocabulary	Moderate	Level 2
44	A	Robust Vocabulary	Moderate	Level 2
45	I	Robust Vocabulary	Moderate	Level 2
46	D	Prefixes, Suffixes, and Roots	Moderate	Level 2
47	F	Prefixes, Suffixes, and Roots	Low	Level 1
48	A	Prefixes, Suffixes, and Roots	Low	Level 1
49	H	Prefixes, Suffixes, and Roots	Moderate	Level 2
50	C	Synonyms and Antonyms	High	Level 2
51	I	Synonyms and Antonyms	Low	Level 1
52	D	Synonyms and Antonyms	High	Level 2
53	H	Synonyms and Antonyms	Moderate	Level 2
54	B	Use Context Clues	Low	Level 1
55	G	Use Context Clues	Moderate	Level 2
Writing Strategies and Conventions				
56	B	Writing Strategies	Moderate	Level 2
57	I	Writing Strategies	Moderate	Level 2
58	C	Writing Strategies	Moderate	Level 2
59	F	Writing Strategies	Moderate	Level 2
60	D	Writing Strategies	Moderate	Level 2
61	I	Writing Strategies	Moderate	Level 2
62	B	Writing Strategies	Moderate	Level 2
63	I	Writing Strategies	Moderate	Level 2
64	C	Writing Strategies	Moderate	Level 2
65	F	Writing Strategies	Moderate	Level 2
66	C	Pronoun-antecedent agreement	Moderate	Level 2
67	G	Words with Inflections -ed and -ing	Moderate	Level 2
68	C	Possessive Nouns	Moderate	Level 2
69	G	Common and Proper Nouns	Moderate	Level 2
70	A	Words with Suffixes -able, -ible, -ness, -ment, -less	Moderate	Level 2
71	H	Homophones	Moderate	Level 2
72	C	Common and Proper Nouns	Moderate	Level 2
73	F	Punctuation Round-up	Moderate	Level 2
74	B	Simple and Compound Sentences	Moderate	Level 2
75	H	Simple and Compound Sentences	Moderate	Level 2

Item Analysis: Mid-Year

		Writing Strategies and Conventions		
Item	Correct Answer	Skill	Cognitive Complexity	Webb's Depth of Knowledge
76	C	Words with VCCV	Moderate	Level 2
77	G	Words with Silent Letters	Moderate	Level 2
78	C	Words with VCCCV	Moderate	Level 2
79	F	Words with VCV	Moderate	Level 2
80	A	Words with Long Vowels and Vowel Digraphs	Moderate	Level 2
Writing to a Prompt				
See page T25 for scoring rubric and model responses.				
Oral Reading Fluency				
See page T7 for Oral Reading Fluency Norms.				

Item Analysis: Mid-Year

Item Analysis: End-of-Year

		Reading Comprehension		
Item	Correct Answer	Skill	Cognitive Complexity	Webb's Depth of Knowledge
1	C	Compare and Contrast	Moderate	Level 2
2	G	Text Structure: Cause and Effect	Moderate	Level 2
3	A	Sequence: Story Events	Moderate	Level 2
4	F	Main Idea and Details	Low	Level 1
5	C	Synonyms and Antonyms	Moderate	Level 2
6	G	Predict Outcomes	High	Level 3
7	*	Plot: Conflict and Resolution	Moderate	Level 2
		* See page T23 for the scoring rubric and model top-scoring responses.		
8	A	Author's Purpose and Perspective	High	Level 3
9	H	Make Inferences	Moderate	Level 2
10	A	Main Idea and Details	Moderate	Level 2
11	G	Use Context Clues	Moderate	Level 2
12	D	Fact and Opinion	Low	Level 1
13	I	Locate Information	Moderate	Level 2
14	B	Locate Information	Moderate	Level 2
15	*	Text Structure: Cause and Effect	Moderate	Level 2
		* See page T23 for the scoring rubric and model top-scoring responses.		
16	F	Figurative Language	High	Level 3
17	A	Figurative Language	High	Level 3
18	I	Use Context Clues	Moderate	Level 2
19	A	Make Inferences	Moderate	Level 2
20	I	Prefixes, Suffixes, and Roots	Low	Level 1
21	A	Locate Information	Moderate	Level 2
22	G	Make Inferences	High	Level 3
23	B	Use Context Clues	Moderate	Level 2
24	I	Text Structure: Sequence	High	Level 3
25	B	Character, Setting, and Plot	Low	Level 1
26	G	Plot: Conflict and Resolution	Moderate	Level 2
27	A	Paraphrase	High	Level 3
28	I	Character's Traits and Motivations	Moderate	Level 2
29	D	Theme	Moderate	Level 2
30	G	Locate Information	Moderate	Level 2
31	A	Fact and Opinion	Moderate	Level 2
32	H	Author's Purpose and Perspective	Moderate	Level 2
33	D	Text Structure: Sequence	High	Level 3
34	G	Predict Outcomes	High	Level 3
35	*	Main Idea and Details	High	Level 3
		* See page T23 for the scoring rubric and model top-scoring responses.		

Item Analysis: End-of-Year

Vocabulary and Word Analysis					
Item	Correct Answer	Skill	Cognitive Complexity	Webb's Depth of Knowledge
36	A	Robust Vocabulary	Moderate	Level 2
37	F	Robust Vocabulary	Moderate	Level 2
38	B	Robust Vocabulary	Moderate	Level 2
39	H	Robust Vocabulary	Moderate	Level 2
40	D	Robust Vocabulary	Moderate	Level 2
41	I	Robust Vocabulary	Moderate	Level 2
42	A	Robust Vocabulary	Moderate	Level 2
43	F	Robust Vocabulary	Moderate	Level 2
44	C	Robust Vocabulary	Moderate	Level 2
45	H	Robust Vocabulary	Moderate	Level 2
46	B	Use Context Clues	Moderate	Level 2
47	G	Prefixes, Suffixes, and Roots	Moderate	Level 2
48	B	Synonyms and Antonyms	Moderate	Level 2
49	F	Synonyms and Antonyms	Moderate	Level 2
50	B	Synonyms and Antonyms	Moderate	Level 2
51	I	Synonyms and Antonyms	Moderate	Level 2
52	B	Synonyms and Antonyms	Moderate	Level 2
53	F	Synonyms and Antonyms	Moderate	Level 2
54	A	Synonyms and Antonyms	Moderate	Level 2
55	G	Prefixes, Suffixes, and Roots	Moderate	Level 2
Writing Strategies and Conventions					
56	C	Writing Strategies	Moderate	Level 2
57	I	Writing Strategies	Moderate	Level 2
58	A	Writing Strategies	Moderate	Level 2
59	G	Writing Strategies	Moderate	Level 2
60	B	Writing Strategies	Moderate	Level 2
61	H	Writing Strategies	Moderate	Level 2
62	A	Writing Strategies	Moderate	Level 2
63	I	Writing Strategies	Moderate	Level 2
64	A	Writing Strategies	Moderate	Level 2
65	F	Writing Strategies	Moderate	Level 2
66	C	Pronouns and Antecedents	Moderate	Level 2
67	H	Contractions and Possessive Pronouns	Moderate	Level 2
68	C	Contractions and Possessive Pronouns	Moderate	Level 2
69	F	Homophones	Moderate	Level 2
70	A	Pronouns and Antecedents	Moderate	Level 2
71	H	Words with Inflections -ed and -ing	Moderate	Level 2
72	A	Common and Proper Nouns	Moderate	Level 2
73	H	Punctuation Round-up	Moderate	Level 2
74	B	Words with Suffixes -able, -ible, -ness, -ment, -less	Moderate	Level 2

Item Analysis: End-of-Year

Writing Strategies and Conventions					
Item	Correct Answer	Skill	Cognitive Complexity	Webb's Depth of Knowledge
75	G	Simple and Compound Sentences	Moderate	Level 2
76	B	Words with Suffixes -ation, -ition, -al, -ial	Moderate	Level 2
77	H	Words with VCV	Moderate	Level 2
78	C	Words with Variant Vowels and Diphthongs	Moderate	Level 2
79	I	Words with Variant Vowels and Diphthongs	Moderate	Level 2
80	D	Words with Prefixes re-, un-, non-	Moderate	Level 2
Writing to a Prompt				
See page T25 for scoring rubric and model responses.				
Oral Reading Fluency				
See page T7 for Oral Reading Fluency Norms.				

*The cognitive complexity of an item is a measure of the level of thinking required of the student.

**Webb's Depth of Knowledge refers to the level of knowledge the item requires of the student. For more information see: Webb, N.L., 1999, Alignment Between Standards and Assessment, University of Wisconsin Center for Educational Research.

Item Analysis: End-of-Year

Scoring Responses to Open-Ended Items

Use the rubrics below to score the open-ended items found in the Reading Comprehension section of the *Benchmark Assessments*.

Short Written Response Rubric	
2 points	• Shows good attention to the task • Clearly based on the text the student read • Includes adequate support or examples • Accurate and complete
1 point	• Shows some attention to the task • Somewhat based on the text the student read • Includes some support or examples • Contains some inaccurate or incomplete details
0 points	• Shows no attention to the task • Not clearly based on the text the student read • Lacks support or examples • Inaccurate and incomplete

Extended Written Response Rubric	
4 points	• Shows complete awareness of the task • Clearly based on the text the student read • Includes effective support or examples • Accurate and complete
3 points	• Shows a general attention to the task • Generally based on the text the student read • Includes mostly adequate support or examples • Mostly accurate and complete
2 points	• Shows some attention to the task • Somewhat based on the text the student read • Some support or examples are inadequate • May contain some inaccuracies or be partially incomplete
1 point	• Shows minimal attention to the task • Minimally based on the text the student read • Includes little support or examples • Contains inaccurate or incomplete details
0 points	• Shows no attention to the task • Not clearly based on the text the student read • Lacks support or examples • Inaccurate and incomplete

Scoring Responses to Open-Ended Items

Model Responses to Open-Ended Items

Below are top-scoring answers for each of the open-ended items found in the Reading Comprehension section of the *Benchmark Assessments*.

Beginning-of-Year

6. Why did the author write this story? Use information and details from the story to explain your answer.

    Model two-point response: The author wrote this story to entertain and to tell about a boy who learned to make a collage from his sister.

12. Why did the author call kudzu, giant toads, and fire ants "invaders"? Use information and details from the article to explain your answer.

    Model two-point response: Invaders arrive somewhere from another place and do harm where they arrive. Kudzu, giant toads, and fire ants arrived in the United States and have harmed their new environments.

18. Describe the purpose of the Indian festival Raksha Bandhan and why it is important to Nina. Use details and information from the story to explain your answer.

    Model four-point response: During the Indian festival of Raksha Bandhan, brothers and sisters declare their love for each other. Brothers promise to protect their sisters, and sisters give their brother a bracelet called a rakhi to symbolize affection. Nina searches for a rakhi for Sanjay to celebrate Raksha Bandhan. Finding a special rakhi is especially important to Nina this year because Sanjay had kept his promise of protection when he defends her against bullies.

Mid-Year

13. How is the conflict in this story resolved? Use details and information from the story to support your answer.

    Model two-point response: Jada is treated the same way she treated Ellie by another girl. Jada realizes she has not been a good friend and apologizes to Ellie.

19. According to the article, what are the effects of exercise? Use details and information from the article to explain your answer.

    Model four-point response: Exercise strengthens your muscles, including your heart. Exercise also gives you more energy; your body does not have to work as hard to move and does not get tired as quickly. Finally, exercise makes you feel good. When you exercise, your body produces a chemical that calms you and makes you feel happier.

35. Why did the author write this article? Use details and information from the article to support your answer.

    Model two-point response: The author wrote this article to show how important robots are to humans. Robots can do jobs that are too dangerous or impossible for humans to do. For example, robots can explore volcanoes on Mars, and humans can't do that.

Model Responses to Open-Ended Items

End-of-Year

7. What is Jasmine's main problem in this story, and how is it solved? Base your answer on details from the story.

   Model two-point response: In this story, Jasmine's main problem occurs when she loses her cat, Ziggy. Jasmine makes posters with a picture of Ziggy and hangs the posters around the neighborhood. Jasmine's main problem is solved when Mrs. Garcia sees Jasmine's posters and finds Ziggy on her porch.

15. According to the article, what are TWO benefits of recycling? Use details and information from the article to explain your answer.

    Model two-point response: According to the article, we should recycle because it creates les garbage. Recycling also keeps us from wasting the earth's trees and metals. It is important to recycle to take care of the earth, ourselves, and our future.

35. Write about the character traits that made Bessie Coleman a good pilot, and explain why those traits are important. Use information from the article to support your answer.

    Model four-point response: Bessie Coleman had several character traits that made her a good pilot. She was strong and determined. Bessie was strong because she was not afraid of flying. In fact, she was fascinated by the stories of the daredevil pilots. It is important for a pilot to be strong because it takes a lot of courage to get in a plane and fly through the air. That could be scary! Bessie's determination was another character trait. When no one thought an African American woman should fly, Bessie kept at it. Bessie's determination helped her continue to learn new things about her career apply them to make herself the best pilot she could be.

Model Responses to Open-Ended Items

Scoring Responses to Writing Prompts

Use the rubric below to score students' responses to the writing prompts on the *Benchmark Assessments*.

	Score of 6	Score of 5	Score of 4	Score of 3	Score of 2	Score of 1
Focus	The writing is completely focused on the topic and has a clear purpose.	The writing is focused on the topic and purpose.	The writing is generally focused on the topic and purpose.	The writing is somewhat focused on the topic and purpose.	The writing is related to the topic but does not have a clear focus.	The writing is not focused on the topic and purpose.
Organization	The ideas in the writing are well-organized and presented in logical order. The paper seems complete to the reader.	The organization of the writing is mostly clear. The paper seems complete.	The organization is mostly clear, but the writing may seem unfinished.	The writing is somewhat organized, but seems unfinished.	There is little organization to the writing.	There is no organization to the writing.
Support	The writing has strong, specific details. The word choices are clear and fresh.	The writing has strong, specific details and clear word choices.	The writing has supporting details and some variety in word choice.	The writing has few supporting details. It needs more variety in word choice.	The writing uses few supporting details and very little variety in word choice.	There are few or no supporting details. The word choices are unclear.
Conventions	The writer uses a variety of sentences. There are few or no errors in grammar, spelling, punctuation, and capitalization.	The writer uses a variety of sentences. There are a few errors in grammar, spelling, punctuation, and capitalization.	The writer uses some variety in sentences. There are a few errors in grammar, spelling, punctuation, and capitalization.	The writer uses simple sentences. There are some errors in grammar, spelling, punctuation, and capitalization.	The writer uses simple sentences. There are many errors in grammar, spelling, punctuation, and capitalization.	The writer uses unclear sentences. There are many errors in grammar, spelling, punctuation, and capitalization.

Model Responses to Writing Prompts

Beginning-of-Year Writing Prompt

Everyone has had a special day that he or she will always remember.

Think about a special day that you will always remember.

Now write a story about that day.

Score 6

This story about meeting a sports player is engaging and meets the requirements for a score of 6. Details are crafted using colorful language ("In fact it was so cold goose bumps were popping up on my skin like popcorn."). The writing is mature and gets the reader involved in the emotions.

It was a phlagmatic hazey December morning. In fact it was so cold goosebumps were popping up on my skin like popcorn. As I was stolling down the street greedily with my five Dollars clenched in my hand, when a collossal gust of wind came and blew my money right out of my hand. I chased after it faster than a rabbit running from a hungry cheetah "Oh no"! it went into a grate. I got down on my hands and knees and reached down "I've got it" I exclaimed but it was not a five dollar bill I pulled out but a Jevon Keerse rookie card! All of a sudden the card started to glow bright green! Then the card started to grow until it was about 6'4". Then it started to grow into the shape of a humin! "Where am I?" Questioned a Deep Voice I was speachless Standing their befor me was Jevon Keerse. Finally

(continued)

Model Responses to Writing Prompts

I gathered up enough breath to say "your in" "oh" he said suspishiously "Well" he said "Would you like to come to watch the super bowl with me" would I ever! I exclaimed as he handed me one ticket. then he called up a taxi to take us to the air port.

After five long harsh hours of flying we were there.

As we entered the staidium we noticed that it was packed like a can of sardines and it was louder than a herd of eliphents stomping their feet the game went scorless until the fourth qurter the seahauks Drove the ball down feild and scored then the steelers had the ball Ben Rothlessburger completed a 48 yard pass to Hines ward they where on the 20 yard line with .35 seconds to go when they completed another pass to Hines ward now they where on the 4 yard line they handed the ball to Jerome Bettis who powered his way in for a touchdown. but they had to go for 2 point conversion to win with 2 seconds on the clock they handed the ball to Jerome Bettis who got it. the crowed went wild every was screaming

After the game Jevon Kearse took me home.

I woke up to the sweet smell of bacon "Mom" I asked did I really go to the super bowl with Jevon Kearse "In your Dreams!"

Score 5

The response to the prompt is about a surprise birthday party. The writing is mature, and ideas are well supported with good details ("A couple of days after the party I asked my Mom if I could have a surprise party too. She said flat out, "No, because if your going to have a surprise party you can't know about it"). The first paragraph tells a lot about the mother's surprise party. This is relevant to the writer's special day, however, more details about the writer's party could have brought this response to a 6.

When it was my Mom's birthday we were thinking of the kind of party for her. So we finally picked it...... a SUPRIZE party! We had it at my Uncle's house. He had a pool, when the party was almost over they pushed my Mom in the pool. I said that I wanted to go in to so they pushed me in the pool too.

A couple days after the party I asked my Mom if I could have a suprize party too. She said flat out, "No because if your going to have a suprize party you can't know about it." Then she said how about a Bratz Doll party. I said "Nooooo Way!" I don't like barbie dolls Bratz dolls or even baby dolls.

When it was my birthday my Mom called my Aunt to come and pick me up early from school to go to the Mall. So my Mom and my family could decorate for my Suprize party. We were at the Mall for at least an hour and a half.

(continued)

Model Responses to Writing Prompts

"We left the Mall and went to the house. She asked me if I wanted ice cream but I said "no thank you". So when we were almost to the door I almost tripped over the water hose. I opened the door and everyone yelled SURPRISE I screamed of course the geanra of the party was butterfly party. It was the best party of my Life."

Score 4

This story meets the prompt's demands by focusing on a moving day. The sequence of events is clear, and simple sentences move the reader through the events and hard work of the day. Details are relevant and give some of the author's feelings about the move ("We did not want to get up early but we had a big day ahead of us.").

My special day is when I moved. I moved because my mom didn't like the place we were at. We lived in New York but my mom wanted to live in Pennsylvania. I had to pack my cloths and my other stuff in big boxes. I had alot of stuff. The boxes were heavy but my dad and I carried them in a big truck. There was a whole bunch of boxes. That day I had to get up early (6p.m). We did not want to get up but we had a big day ahead of us. After we put all the boxes into the truck my arms were so sore. It was time to hit the road and move to Pennsylvania. We had no car we usialy walked. We had to drive in the truck It was a long ride, I went to sleep. When we got there I saw my new house. It looked nice but not that nice. We had to unload the truck and carry all the boxes into the house it was pretty late about 5 p.m. After we put the boxes in the hous we checked out our new room and they were so nice. Then we

(continued)

Model Responses to Writing Prompts

had to go to our grandmothers house and we had to sleep there while my mom and dad were unloadin the boxes. They came home late I was sleeping. The next day we went to our new house and I met 3 new friends. That is my special day.

Score 3

The writing focuses on spending a special day at an amusement park. A few ideas about the rides are developed, but there is a looseness to the writer's style ("An then I went on a cool ride. I do not remember what it was called."). Word choice and sentence construction are both simple. Repetition is seen in the four uses of "I will never forget..." in the final section.

One time it was my brithday and we all went to Wet-en Wild you know me and my family. An Then I went on a cool ride. I do not remember what it was called But it was so much fun.

Then after I went on that ride and Got off. I found another ride I wanted to ride. It was called The black hole. I went with my dad on That ride. but I Think that was the only ride I went with him on at That time.

Then I went on a ride That was so much fun. I Think it was called hiller slide. it is not scary. But it was a really long slide. That is why they call it The biller slide.

I went on it a lot of times. I mean alot. I loved

(continued)

Model Responses to Writing Prompts

That ride. There was a skieing ride To But I was to afraid to go on That ride. any way I had fun There and That all That maters and That day I will never forget I mean never forget. That is a day I will never forget even when I get to my old ages. I still will never fget Those days!

Score 2

This slim response only slightly addresses the prompt. There are few supporting ideas to elaborate on the special day in Orlando. It is an example of a "too-brief" response. After telling the hotel's name, the writer only provides details about eating breakfast, taking a walk, and going to the pool.

> The day I will always remember is going to a modern hotel in Orlanda Florida it is called Coronado Springs. The first thing we did was go eat breakfest then we went for a walk at last we went to the pool That is what I did on my special day that I will always remember.

Model Responses to Writing Prompts

> **Score 1**
> This response only minimally addresses the prompt. There are few details to support the idea of having fun at an amusement park. The brief piece also includes too much repetition (e.g., "fun" is used four times and "family" is used three times).

A special place that I always remember is Disney world because it was fun rides and fun games and having fun with my family. Disneyworld is a place I will always remember because it was the funest place I ever had and my family. Disneyworld is my best place to have fun with your family. That's why Disney world is a place I will always remember.

Mid-Year Writing Prompt

Most of us have a favorite game or hobby that we enjoy.

Think about a game or hobby that you enjoy.

Now write to explain what you like about that game or hobby.

Score 6

This piece is cohesively organized and clearly addresses the prompt. The ideas are effectively supported with salient details. A command of language and the use of varied sentence structures enhance this response. The first sentence is an example of this ("'Perfecto! I feel like Van Gough already!'"). Each new main idea cleverly flows from the one before.

"Perfecto! I feel like Van Gogh already!" Many of you may be wondering, what is my favorite hobby? Well, wait no longer, it is Art. I shall now inform you why I like this subject so much.

I'd have to say my favorite form of Art would be freestyle, and with a pencil. Its easy to make mistakes, and with a pencil I have a choice: Fix it, or create it into something new. With a pencil, I can create a horse into a unicorn, a house into a castle, a broom into a witch on a broom, without messing up the whole thing. Its also neater, and when I'm finished, I either color it in, or it's back to the drawing board to make a new masterpiece.

Quick! Before the paint dries, I have to tell you something: I also like to paint! I definitely don't like to paint as much as I do freestyle. With paint, you have limits. Too much paint and your art is ruined, too little and it isn't as good. It takes

(continued)

takes a long time. I mean, if I were to do a log cabin, I'd have to do brown, black line, brown, black line, and so on. But in the end it won't look like a masterpiece. Okay, let me tell you why I do like it. I love the colors. Orange, pink, green, teal, everything! I like to mix them, and see what they look like. Also, since I enjoy doing abstract work, paint is a good tool for that. With freestyle, it takes awhile, but with paint, a few dots, lines, waves, circles, and you've got a work of art!

Now, don't let this leak out, but I also enjoy markers. The only fault is that markers, well, the ink runs. I put a dot, and most of the time it's too big. I enjoy markers when I color things in, like grass, or the sun, or flowers. I also love the variety and selection of colors that markers have, too. I usually keep markers handy for illustrations for school projects, or at home. Whenever I see markers at the store, I'll ask for them. Then, I'll stash them away until I need them.

Well, time is coming to a close. I also love art because it gives me a feeling I can create anything, and I can! With practice, of course. Oil pastels, paints, colored pencils, markers, pencils, everything! I like them all, those I wrote about just happen to be my favorite. I can see it now: 'Baillie Ward, the new Van Gough!' Be sure to check the art museums if you ever get the chance to go.

Model Responses to Writing Prompts

Score 5

The response meets the requirements of the prompt. All of the details are focused on why the writer enjoys sketching. The sequence of ideas could be better. Sentences are generally simple in structure with a few lapses in punctuation.

My favorite hobby is sketching. My mom says my drawings are really good and when I get older, I will become a famous artist. When I sketch, I listen to music. Music sometimes helps me think of a person in the pictures expression. If the person is happy, I would listen to a positive song. If the person is sad I listen to a sad song.

Ever since I was 8, I have been drawing stuff like the Medieval times and Japenese Anime. Drawing the Medieval Times is fun. I draw castles, Knights, Jesters, Kings, Queens, Knights fighting dragons, and other things that are based in that time. Drawing Japenese Anime is fun but way different. Drawing Japenese Anime can be extremely difficult. I have been drawing Japenese Anime more than the Medieval times. The way I study Japenese Anime is through watching a Japenese Animation shows on television like Avatar, the last

(continued)

air bender and Pokemon.

When I started drawing, I would get a picture of my favorite singer and study it for a minute. Then I would try and draw it.

I have been drawing since I was 6 and I want to be an artist when I get older. I think I get my talents from my mom.

Score 4

The writer of this response supports ideas with some specific details, logically using transition signals and paragraphing. Word choice is adequate and the introduction and closing are effective.

My favorite Hobby is cheerleading. I like cheerleading Because you get to be with your friends. Next is you get a lot of excersice.

To begin with, cheerleading is cool Because you get to be with your friends One time when I wanted a friend I told my mom "can I got to cheerleading practice Because all my friends are there" "Yes" she explained. So I went to cheerleading Practice. And I got to Play with all my friends. Another time when My friends called me and they wanted to come over so they did then they had to go to cheerleading Practice. So I was alone then it was time for me to go so I went and got to Play with them.

In addition, My second reason I like cheerleading is Because it gives me exersice. One time when we were Practicing And I was sweating and sweating and I Lost 5 Pounds it was a real exercise. Another time when Me and my friend were doing a cheer and me and a friend were

(continued)

Model Responses to Writing Prompts

so tired that I couldn't do anything not even eat. So I went home and took a nap for 3 hours.

    In conclusion, My favorite hobby is Cheerleading Because I get to Be with friends and I get a lot of exersice. in the future I will be cheering my but off for the game.

Score 3

This response relates to the prompt by focusing on four games. Some contradictory details are included that do not contribute to the idea of these games being fun ("But what I dont like about tag is that when you run your body part(s) hurt.") The response demonstrates some organization but lacks a closing to tie these 4 games together.

What I like about 7up is that its fun and not chalenging, so you dont get in a fight. Its also really really fun to play. Thats why I like 7up

What I like about Tag is it's fun. You also get alot of exersize. But what I dont like about tag is that when you run your body part(s) hurt. These are the resons why I do and dont like Tag

The reson why I love Connect four is because its quiet and fun to play anytime, anywhere. Its also two player. So you have to take turns if thur is more than two people. Or they could just be on your team.

The reson I like Scrabble is because you get to choose so many words. It's also really fun. Then again its also hard. But sometimes it's easy.

Model Responses to Writing Prompts

Score 2

This writing loosely meets the prompt's requirements by mentioning some enjoyable details of basketball. However, the main idea is not clear, and some details are personal feelings that don't support the prompt ("I cross people over and want to be the first person picked instead of the last one."). Omitted words and incomplete sentences affect readability ("I like for my friend pass me the ball I'm sor they want me to pass the ball.").

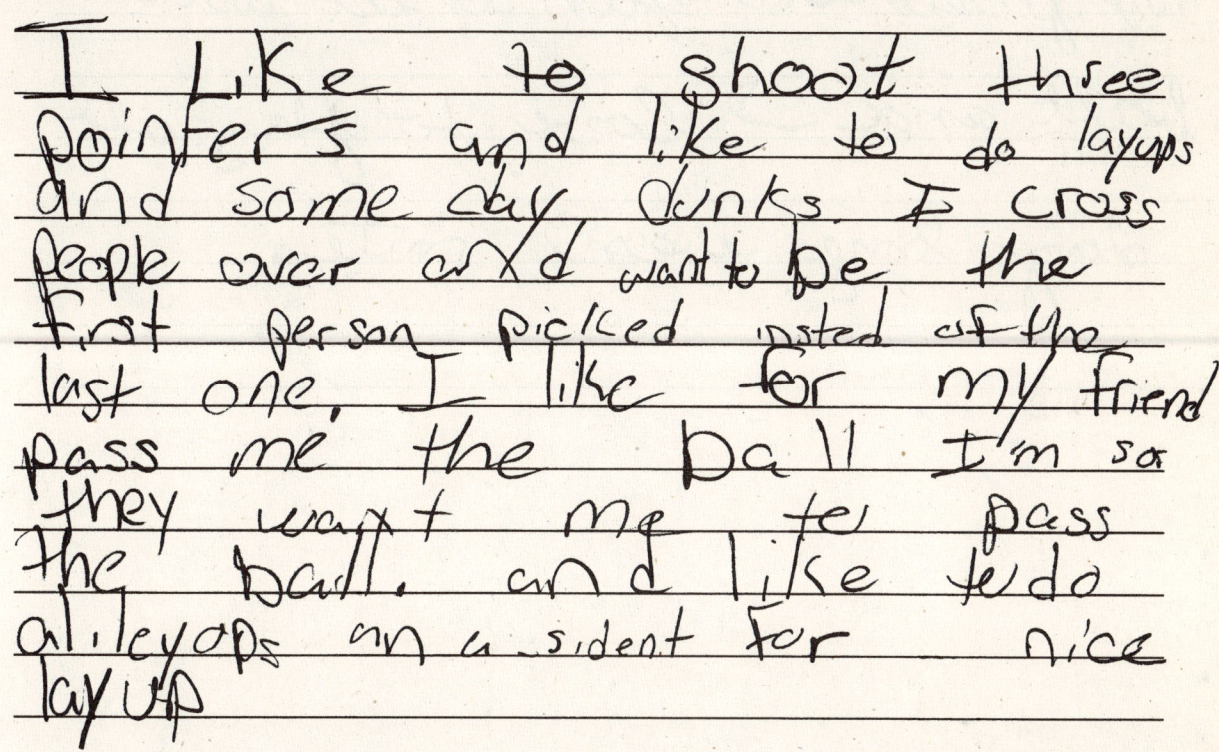

I like to shoot three pointers and like to do layups and some day dunks. I cross people over and want to be the first person picked insted of the last one. I like for my friend pass me the ball I'm sor they want me to pass the ball. and like to do alleyops an a sident for nice layup

Model Responses to Writing Prompts

Score 1

The writing is the beginning of a response, but no elaboration of ideas or details is included. The favorite game is identified as football, which the writer says he loves to play all day long.

my favorite game is foot ball and I love to play all day long even nite.

End-of-Year Writing Prompt

Everyone has learned how to do new things.

Think about a time when you learned how to do something new.

Now write a story about a time when you learned how to do something new.

Score 6

This is a well-paced story about learning to ride a bike that uses good details to keep the reader interested. The story employs a variety of sentence structures with easy transitions ("So my dad went into his toolbox, pulled out a wrench and got to work."). The details about sibling rivalry are an added bonus for the reader as the older sister teases the younger novice ("My sister laughed even harder. I wanted to call it quits, but I was determined.").

Have you ever learned how to do something new? Well I have, it was one of the best memories of my life!

When I was young, I didn't know how to ride a bike. My sister was able to. She teased and teased me about it. The next day my dad came home with a bike. (With training wheels, because I was only about 3) My dad was helping me so much. I was scared at first, but then I got the hang of it. Then my sister didn't have training wheels anymore, she teased me about that also.

I told my dad, "I want to ride a bike without training wheels. He said "Okay." So my dad went into his toolbox, pulled out a wrench and got to work. When he was done he said, "Hop on!" So I did. I tried to ride without help. I fell, and my

(continued)

Model Responses to Writing Prompts

sister laughed. I wanted to just get up and shove her, but before I could my dad ran over, picked up the bike and said, "Get on, and do it again!" So I got back on and rode around. I didn't fall! I was so happy. Until I had to stop. BANG!!! I ran straight into a tree. My sister laughed even harder. I wanted to call it quits, but I was determaned.

 I got right back on the bike and tought myself how to stop and before I knew it, I was equal with my sister. We rode around together, raced, play tag on our bikes. It was so much fun.

 That was one of the best days of my life. Exept the fact that I fell twice, I was so happy!

Score 5

While not hitting the topic directly, this response is organized with creative details. Transitions move the story along, and there are a variety of sentence styles. Some details are confusing, but overall the description makes the response unique and interesting.

WoW! did you see how fast I ran I can't belive it I made It home before 3:50 Now thats a record!

Okay I will run here at my corner to the end of the block and back. I ran so hard All I saw was a blur and my neighbors looked at me questionally like (what has gotten into that boy) they thought. But I couldn't belive that I ran so fast I am excited.

So then I started to practice practice practice because hey you know the old saying "practice makes perfect. But those are not the words I live by but any who I practiced 7 days a week from 1:00am to 5:00pm and man I sure be as tired as a man who works 24-7 lifting and bending picking bending picking up boxes om metal 5,000 pound sledge hammers.

Then one Tuesday while I was at VPAA Running around the track passing everybody The track team coach called me over I was panting real hard Then he told me, "I saw you

(continued)

Model Responses to Writing Prompts

running and man you are amazing I would like you to join the 8th Grade track team" Suddenly I froze because a 4th grader like me on an 8th grade track team "Okay" I replied But the 8th graders were not competable but the meet was tomorrow and I was anxious but ready.

When I got to the track team meet the coach said "where were you, we could have lost in a blink of an eye" I camly replied "I was helping my mom with something." So then the race was on I was number 10 I said out loud "Every man for himself"!!! Then the person shot his gun and I took of running like a speedy bullet but I was in last place so I said "Oh no you dont" Then I hit my nitro and everybody in the stand were yelling "go number 10" and the 8th graders were surprised when I passed all of them then I was so tired. I ran all the way to the finish line I came in 1st place gold metal and everything.

I went home plopped on the chair my dog got mad I sat in his spot. Mom asked me "where" I huffed in "Theolyn So This why I tell the story of when I learned something new.

Score 4

A fun opening starts off this response and effective use of language keeps the reader's interest ("I was dying of boredom.") Better organization and a stronger conclusion could have raised the score on this response.

Splash!!! My apolagees about that. I just did a front flip in my deep pool. That remind's me of the time I did my first front flip. It was a hot day. A perfect time to take a dip in the refreshing pool. As a swan around in the pool for a while I was dying of bordem. I wished for a new way of jumping into the swimming hole. And I knew was ready for front flips. But as I was thinking of the dangers I decided to jump. When I got out of the blow cristal water I feeit the mealed sun beating on me. as I stood far away from the pool I felt ready. I ran torwd the pool with all my might. When was at the edge of the water hole I jumpt. Then culd into a ball. Then splash I made it!

Model Responses to Writing Prompts

Score 3

This response addresses the prompt and is clearly organized with a beginning, middle, and end. It is enhanced with appropriate details. Engaging language is attempted ("... harder then a turtles shell."), but weak conventions of writing, such as scarce punctuation and spelling errors, interfere with readability.

one day I wanted to Learn how to ride a bike so my sister teached me how to ride one at first I couldn't even get on it. When I findly got on it I crashed into a mailbox Then I got up and I rode it but first I had to know how to stop, it was harder Then a turtles shell. but I didn't know how to turn I bumped right into stopsing. There is something I still didn't know how to do and that was controwtouling the bike. I crash my new bike right into my moms new car and got a broken leg and a arm but it hill in to mouths and I Learn how to ride a bike, but there was one Promble I didn't have a bike any more after that bike crash I got into my bike was damige. I had to wait a week for my bike by The time it was fixed I had to relearn how

(continued)

Model Responses to Writing Prompts

to ride a bike again because
I forgot how to ride a bike
and I had to get more engery
I wasn't happy but I could
never go riding with my friends
if I don't know how to ride a bike
and any ways I had no choose.
and That was something I Learned
how to do that was new to me.

Score 2

This slim response focuses on learning something new, the Disco Line Dance. The details tell when the dance was learned and where it was performed but the reader does not get a picture of exactly what the dance looks like. A higher score would require this relevant information.

When I was in third grade and fourth grade, I learned how to do the Disco line Dance, square dance, and a lot more that I cant remember. When we learned the Disco line dance 3 or 4 people from each 3rd grade class had to do the dance on grandparents day, and I was one of them!

Score 1

This response only minimally meets the prompt. It includes details about playing a game ("Champyon") but provides no information explaining what type of game this is. Learning something new is never mentioned in the piece. Including these details would have raised this response to a better score since conventions of writing are adequate.

One day I was tring to find my friend Amber, I found her playing Champyon. The next day _____ _____ and _____ were playing too. When I saw them play I deciede to play too. When I played Champyon I mett so new friends like _____ and _____. I think Champyon is a exciting and energetic game and I hope I can play it agan.

Model Responses to Writing Prompts

HARCOURT SCHOOL PUBLISHERS
STORYtown

Grade 4 Benchmark Assessment
Beginning-of-Year

Name _____ Date _____

Performance Summary

	Student Score
READING	
Reading Comprehension	
Multiple-Choice Items	_____/32
Short-Response Open-Ended Item	_____/2
Short-Response Open-Ended Item	_____/2
Extended-Response Open-Ended Item	_____/4
Vocabulary and Word Analysis	_____/20
Total Student Reading Score	_____/60
WRITING	
Writing Strategies and Conventions	_____/25
Writing Prompt	_____/6
ORAL READING FLUENCY	
Passage 1	_____ Words Correct Per Minute
Passage 2	_____ Words Correct Per Minute

(Bubble in the appropriate performance level.)

Reading

Below Basic	Basic (On-Level)	Proficient (On-Level)	Advanced
1–35	36–45	46–55	56–60
○	○	○	○

Writing Conventions

Below Basic	Basic (On-Level)	Proficient (On-Level)	Advanced
1–10	11–15	16–19	20–25
○	○	○	○

Writing Prompt

Below Basic	Basic (On-Level)	Proficient (On-Level)	Advanced
1–2	3–4	5	6
○	○	○	○

Oral Reading Fluency

25th Percentile	50th Percentile	75th Percentile	90th Percentile
68 WCPM	94 WCPM	119 WCPM	145 WCPM
○	○	○	○

Grateful acknowledgment is made to The Cricket Magazine Group, a division of Carus Publishing Company for permission to reprint "Sandy Skyscrapers to Clay Cobras" by Julie Brooks Hiller, P.G., illustrated by Karen Dugan from *Spider* Magazine, April 2006. Text copyright © 2006 by Carus Publishing Company; illustrations copyright © 2006 by Karen Dugan.

Copyright © by Harcourt, Inc.

All rights reserved. No part of this publication may be reproduced or transmitted in any form or by any means, electronic or mechanical, including photocopy, recording, or any information storage and retrieval system, without permission in writing from the publisher.

Permission is hereby granted to individuals using the corresponding student's textbook or kit as the major vehicle for regular classroom instruction to photocopy entire pages from this publication in classroom quantities for instructional use and not for resale. Requests for information on other matters regarding duplication of this work should be addressed to School Permissions and Copyrights, Harcourt, Inc., 6277 Sea Harbor Drive, Orlando, Florida 32887-6777. Fax: 407-345-2418.

HARCOURT and the Harcourt Logo are trademarks of Harcourt, Inc., registered in the United States of America and/or other jurisdictions.

Printed in the United States of America

ISBN 10 0-15-358768-7   ISBN 13 978-0-15-358768-9

1 2 3 4 5 6 7 8 9 10 073 16 15 14 13 12 11 10 09 08 07

If you have received these materials as examination copies free of charge, Harcourt School Publishers retains title to the materials and they may not be resold. Resale of examination copies is strictly prohibited and is illegal.

Possession of this publication in print format does not entitle users to convert this publication, or any portion of it, into electronic format.

Read the story "An Art Project" before answering Numbers 1 through 6.

An Art Project

As Kasara and her brother, Darryl, strolled to school, Kasara stopped to pick up a feather, and a few minutes later, a leaf from an oak tree.

"What are you doing, Kasara?" Darryl inquired.

"I'm collecting objects to create a collage," Kasara explained.

"What's a collage?" Darryl asked.

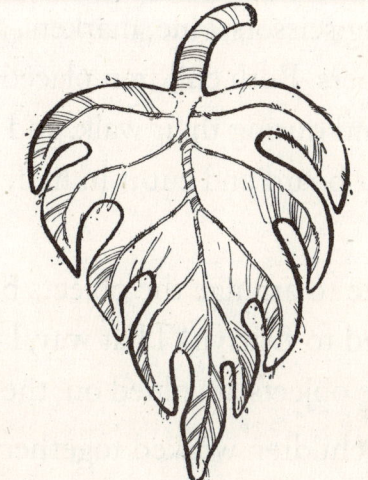

"Collage is a kind of art in which you arrange a lot of different kinds of objects and scraps on a piece of paper or cardboard, and then you glue them in place," Kasara explained. "What you get is a unique collection of colors and textures. My class has made collages a couple of times already this year."

"Other than feathers and leaves and scraps, what kinds of objects do you use?" Darryl asked.

"You can use just about anything you want. Caps of soda bottles, plastic packaging, old postage stamps, and greeting cards are some things I've used, and this time, I'm also going to cut words and pictures out of old magazines and newspapers. You can even draw or paint on a collage if you want," said Kasara.

"That sounds like fun. Can I make a collage too?" Darryl asked.

"Sure. We can work on it together after we finish our homework tonight," answered Kasara.

During the rest of the walk to school, Darryl looked for objects he could use to create his collage, and he continued to look for more things as he walked home that afternoon.

He found a piece of string, some shiny, colorful paper, and even some bark from a tree.

Kasara laughed as she watched him. "You're excited about this project, aren't you?" she asked.

"Yeah! I have lots of ideas about how I want my collage to look," Darryl said.

The children arrived at home and first did their homework. Then they gathered the art supplies they would need to make the collage, including scissors, glue, markers, and a stack of old magazines and newspapers. Both children placed on the table all the objects they had found during their walk, and then Kasara unrolled a large piece of poster board and cut it in half; half for herself and half for her brother.

"I like to arrange the objects before I glue anything down," Kasara explained to Darryl. "That way, I can make changes if I want to, but once the objects are glued on, the collage is pretty permanent."

The children worked together for the rest of the evening. After a few hours, they had glued everything in place and set the collages aside for the glue to dry thoroughly. The next morning, they each went to check on their completed projects.

Darryl looked at his sister and grinned. "You're the official art instructor of the family now. What will tomorrow's art project be?" he asked. She laughed and ruffled his hair.

Name _____

Benchmark Assessment

Beginning-of-Year

▶ Now answer Numbers 1 through 6. Base your answers on the story "An Art Project."

1. Why did Kasara think that Darryl was excited about making a collage?
    - Ⓐ He started his collage the minute he finished his homework.
    - Ⓑ He told Kasara that he had lots of ideas about making a collage.
    - Ⓒ He started looking everywhere for objects for his collage.
    - Ⓓ He asked Kasara if he could make a collage when she made hers.

2. Read these sentences from the story.

    > "I like to arrange the objects before I glue anything down," Kasara explained to Darryl. "That way, I can make changes if I want to, but once the objects are glued on, the collage is pretty permanent."

    What does *permanent* mean?
    - Ⓕ flexible
    - Ⓖ unchangeable
    - Ⓗ interesting
    - Ⓘ perfect

3. Which of these things did Darryl probably do as he worked on his collage?
    - Ⓐ told Kasara a better way to arrange her objects on the poster board
    - Ⓑ arranged his objects before he glued any of them down
    - Ⓒ made a few changes to his collage after he had glued down the objects
    - Ⓓ removed objects after he had arranged all the objects

Reading Comprehension

3

GO ON

© Harcourt • Grade 4

Name _____

Benchmark Assessment
Beginning-of-Year

4. According to the story, what does Darryl think of his sister?

   Ⓕ She is a good teacher.

   Ⓖ She likes to learn from others.

   Ⓗ She most enjoys working alone.

   Ⓘ She likes to try new things more than he does.

5. Which MOST LIKELY happened in the days after the story ended?

   Ⓐ Kasara will teach Darryl how to do other kinds of art.

   Ⓑ Darryl will tell Kasara he does not enjoy making art.

   Ⓒ The collages Kasara and Darryl made will fall apart.

   Ⓓ Kasara will decide she would rather work by herself.

READ THINK EXPLAIN

6. Why did the author write this story? Use details and information from the story to explain your answer.

   _____
   _____
   _____
   _____
   _____
   _____
   _____
   _____

Reading Comprehension

GO ON

Name _____

Benchmark Assessment

Beginning-of-Year

▶ Read the story "Uninvited Guests" before answering Numbers 7 through 12.

Uninvited Guests

Our country has been invaded! However, it's not people who are the invaders. It's plants and animals.

These plants and animals are native to other parts of the world and were brought to North America. When transplanted out of their native environment, they can damage their new homes. They cause disease, wipe out native plants and animals, and cost a lot of money to control or eliminate.

What are some of the plants and animals that are causing trouble, and how did they get here? One such plant is called kudzu, a vine that was brought to the United States from Japan in 1876.

At first, kudzu was a well-liked plant, admired for the color of its flowers. It also appeared to be useful because it could keep soil from washing away. However, the vine grows very fast; too fast. Kudzu covers land that people need for forestry and farming. It can kill trees and shrubs by uprooting them or blocking out sunlight.

Similarly, a problematic animal, native to Central and South America, is the giant toad. The giant toad grows to be six inches long. (That's long for a toad.) The people who brought this toad to the United States wanted it to eat certain bugs that were eating crops.  Unfortunately, the toads have many babies. These toads are also very poisonous. Other animals that eat the toads can become sick or may even die.

Reading Comprehension

GO ON

© Harcourt • Grade 4

A non-native insect that is very troublesome is the fire ant. Not only can it damage crops, it also protects other insects that hurt the crops. Fire ants have actually destroyed roads by removing the dirt from under the road bed.

When fire ants are disturbed, they swarm and bite. The ant bites hurt, itch, and burn. If the ants are swarming, it is possible for a person to be stung hundreds of times.

Plants and animals that are not native to this environment can be pests. It can cost a lot of money to get rid of them. They can destroy crops and forests. They can also harm the plants and animals that are native to an area. It is better to think carefully before transplanting a plant or animal from its native environment to a new one.

Name _____

Now answer Numbers 7 through 12. Base your answers on the article "Uninvited Guests."

7. Which words from the article have almost the SAME meaning?
   - Ⓕ live in, invade
   - Ⓖ troublesome, harmful
   - Ⓗ native, new
   - Ⓘ wipe out, eliminate

8. What is the MAIN reason the author believes that kudzu is a pest?
   - Ⓐ It takes over land and plants.
   - Ⓑ It is not useful to people.
   - Ⓒ It costs a lot of money to control.
   - Ⓓ It makes animals sick when they eat it.

9. In what way are kudzu and the giant toad ALIKE?
   - Ⓕ Both are known to cause diseases.
   - Ⓖ Both can make people itch or burn.
   - Ⓗ Both can make animals sick if they are eaten.
   - Ⓘ Both were brought to the United States to be helpful.

Name _____

Benchmark Assessment

Beginning-of-Year

10. Read this sentence from the article.

    It is better to think carefully before transplanting a species from its native environment to a new one.

    What does *transplanting* mean?

    Ⓐ planting different things at different times
    Ⓑ planting the same thing more than one time
    Ⓒ moving something from one place to another
    Ⓓ being able to be moved from one place to another

11. What is this article MOSTLY about?

    Ⓕ plants and animals that damage crops
    Ⓖ plants and animals that come from other places and do harm
    Ⓗ plants and animals that have become popular in the United States
    Ⓘ plants and animals that cause people to feel sick

Reading Comprehension

GO ON

Name _____

Benchmark Assessment
Beginning-of-Year

READ THINK EXPLAIN

12. Why did the author call kudzu, giant toads, and fire ants "invaders"? Use information and details from the article to explain your answer.

_____
_____
_____
_____
_____
_____
_____

Reading Comprehension

9

GO ON

Read the story "Sanjay's Rakhi" before answering Numbers 13 through 18.

Sanjay's Rakhi

Nina and her mother perused the marketplace, examining rows and rows of tables groaning with the weight of homemade food, jewelry, and paper cut-outs. Stopping at one table, Nina's mother held up a bracelet made of thread. "What about this rakhi for Sanjay?" she said.

Nina looked at the rakhi in her mother's hand. "It's nice," she said. "But this Raksha Bandhan, I want Sanjay's rakhi to be special. I'm going to keep looking." Nina turned back to the display of rakhis.

Tomorrow was Raksha Bandhan. This festival was always held on a full moon in August. Raksha Bandhan was a holiday just for siblings. On this day, brothers and sisters declared their affection and devotion for each other with words, rituals, and small gifts. Sisters wished their brothers well. Brothers promised to protect sisters from harm.

Nina had always loved celebrating Raksha Bandhan with her brother Sanjay. Each year they would look forward to the holiday, the special dishes, and the presents. But this year the festival meant more to her than it had in the past.

Sanjay was walking home from school one day that spring when he saw Nina surrounded by a group of older students. At first he was glad that she had made some new friends. But when he approached them, he saw that one of the boys held Nina's schoolbooks. Papers and pencils were scattered on the ground, and Nina was crouching on the ground, crying.

Sanjay pushed the boys aside and knelt down beside Nina. "Come on, let's go home," he said gently. He helped her gather her things, and with a scathing glance at the bullies, he led her away. No one from school had teased his little sister since then.

Raksha Bandhan was a time for honoring the bond between brothers and sisters, but until now, Nina had treated it like any other fun holiday. Since Sanjay had stood up for her, she understood what it meant to him to promise his protection. The festival now held more significance for Nina than ever. She had decided to buy Sanjay the most beautiful rakhi she could afford.

Nina wandered over to another table and looked at the rakhis. Right away one caught her eye. This rakhi had a band made of brightly colored thread. In the center was a sunburst of gold paper and turquoise beads. She grinned when the salesman told her how much the rakhi cost.

"Mom, I found it!" Nina cried. "Look what I'm going to give Sanjay!"

Name _____

Benchmark Assessment

Beginning-of-Year

▶ Now answer Numbers 13 through 18. Base your answers on the story "Sanjay's Rakhi."

13. What does Nina decide in the story?
    - Ⓐ why she wants to buy a special rakhi
    - Ⓑ which rakhi to buy for her brother
    - Ⓒ what gifts she will receive at the festival
    - Ⓓ what dishes she will cook for the festival

14. Where does MOST of the story take place?
    - Ⓕ at Nina and Sanjay's house
    - Ⓖ at the market
    - Ⓗ at the festival
    - Ⓘ at Nina and Sanjay's school

15. Which of the following will MOST LIKELY happen next?
    - Ⓐ Nina will buy the rakhi for Sanjay.
    - Ⓑ Nina will continue to shop for rakhis.
    - Ⓒ Nina will ask her mother to buy the rakhi.
    - Ⓓ Nina will promise to protect Sanjay.

Reading Comprehension

GO ON

Name _____

16. Which word BEST describes Nina in this story?
    F upset
    G thankful
    H unsure
    I helpful

17. Which BEST describes the theme of the story?
    A A gift is only good if it costs a lot of money.
    B Preparing for a festival takes a lot of time.
    C Sometimes people need help in picking the perfect gift.
    D Giving gifts is as rewarding as receiving them.

Name _____

Benchmark Assessment

Beginning-of-Year

18. Describe the purpose of the Indian festival Raksha Bandhan and why it is important to Nina. Use details and information from the story to explain your answer.

_____
_____
_____
_____
_____
_____
_____
_____
_____
_____
_____
_____
_____

Reading Comprehension

GO ON

Read the article "Sandy Skyscrapers to Clay Cobras" before answering Numbers 19 through 23.

Sandy Skyscrapers to Clay Cobras

by Julie Brooks Hiller, P.G.
art by Karen Dugan

What in the world is coating your sneakers? Is *silt* stuck between the zigzags? Is *clay* caked to your laces? Is *sand* scraping your toes? *Gravel* gouging your heel? A soil scientist knows the difference between silt, clay, sand, and gravel. Do you?

It's simple, if you remember it's only a matter of size.

Sand and gravel are made of different-sized pieces of rock. Gravel is made up of coarser rock about the size of a marble or larger. Sand is tiny, fine, and gritty, about the size of a freckle—perfect for building sandy skyscrapers at the shore!

Silt and clay are also made of rock, but the pieces are so tiny that you can't see them with the naked eye. So how can you tell the difference without a microscope? Your fingers can figure it out. Soil with lots of silt in it feels creamy, like buttery icing. Soil with lots of clay in it feels sticky and rolls between your fingers like modeling clay—perfect for creating clay cobras!

Most folks have a mixture of gravel, sand, clay, and silt in their backyards. What's in yours? If you live on a beach, you may have only one type of soil—sand. If you live inland, perhaps you'll find all four types. Wherever you live, if you enjoy getting messy, you'll have fun performing this experiment to find out. It's as easy as pie—*mud* pie.

What You'll Need:

1-quart bucket or bowl
hand shovel
1 cup water
finely meshed wire sieve
1 gallon water for washing playclothes

What to Do:

1. Use the hand shovel to dig a soil sample from the yard. (Ask an adult where you may dig.)
2. Fill the bucket or bowl half full with soil.

3. Add 1/2 cup water and mix with your hands until the thick mud sticks together like a giant meatball. Add more water if the soil is still too dry. Be careful not to add too much water. It will make the soil soupy.

4. Rub your fingers together and feel the soil texture. Do you feel rock pieces about as big as marbles? If so, you have gravel in your soil. Does it feel gritty, like sandpaper? If so, you have sand in your soil. Does it coat your skin and feel creamy, like buttery icing? If so, you have silt in your soil. Does it feel sticky, and can you roll it into a snake shape? If so, you have clay in your soil.

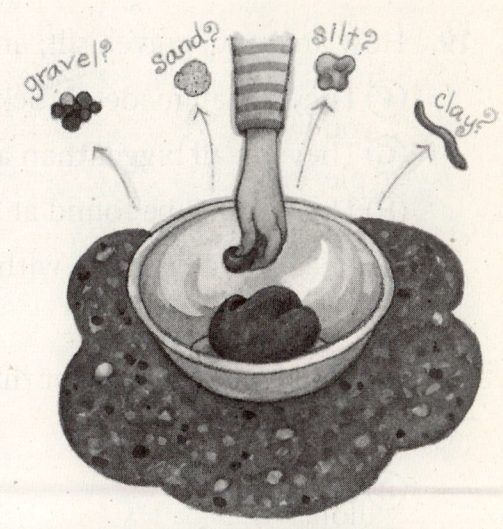

5. To better see the sand and gravel, put the soil into the sieve and rinse the silt and clay away with water until only rock pieces are left. What colors do you see? Are the pieces rounded or angular?

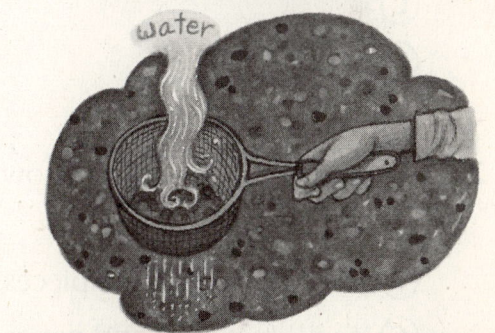

6. Congratulations! You've just completed tests done by real soil scientists, and you've discovered what kinds of soil are in your own backyard! (Don't forget to wash up before going into your house!)

Name _____

Benchmark Assessment

Beginning-of-Year

▶ Now answer Numbers 19 through 23. Base your answers on the article "Sandy Skyscrapers to Clay Cobras."

19. How are sand, gravel, silt, and clay ALIKE?
    - F They are all made of rock.
    - G They are all bigger than a freckle.
    - H They can all be found at or near a beach.
    - I They can all be seen without a microscope.

20. In which step do you test the soil by feeling it?
    - A 1
    - B 3
    - C 4
    - D 6

21. According to the article, how do you know if you have gravel in your soil?
    - F It will contain rock pieces.
    - G It will feel like sand paper.
    - H It will coat your skin.
    - I It will feel sticky.

Reading Comprehension

GO ON

Name _____

22. Which sentence from the article is a FACT and not an opinion?

  (A) "Soil with lots of silt in it feels creamy, like buttery icing."

  (B) "A soil scientist knows the difference between silt, clay, sand, and gravel."

  (C) "Wherever you live, if you enjoy getting messy, you'll have fun performing this experiment to find out."

  (D) "Sand is tiny, fine, and gritty, about the size of a freckle— perfect for building sandy skyscrapers at the shore!"

23. Which part of the directions is MOST important to follow?

  (F) mixing the right amount of water in with the soil

  (G) making sure the skin is fully coated with soil

  (H) making sure the snake shape is long

  (I) using the right kind of bucket

Read the journal entry "Jeff's Journal" before answering Numbers 24 through 29.

Jeff's Journal

September 2

When I grow up I want to be a chef. My friends think I am crazy; they say cooking is for girls. I don't care what they say. I watch cooking shows on television, and many of the stars on those shows are men.

I've already learned a lot about what it takes to be a chef. The library had some books about cooking. One book said that, in French, the word "chef" means boss or chief in French. One day, I will be the boss of a kitchen.

Another book explained all about the different jobs for the people who prepare food. A restaurant kitchen is a busy place! Prep cooks clean the food, slice fruits and vegetables, and chop other ingredients. Pastry specialists prepare dough for baked goods and arrange fancy desserts just before they are served. Cooks on the "hot line" prepare fish and meat entrees that are served hot to waiting customers.

Apparently becoming a lead chef is not easy. You must go to school and practice for years. In college I plan to study the culinary arts and learn about becoming a chef. They teach you how to prepare food, cook different dishes, and how to make food appear attractive when it is served. When I finish college, I would like to study more in another country. Right now, my first choice is Italy, but I might change my mind when I get older.

Both my mom and dad love to cook, and they let me help them shop, plan meals, and even do some of the cooking. Maybe that's why my goal is to be a chef when I grow up.

Name _____

Benchmark Assessment
Beginning-of-Year

▶ Now answer Numbers 24 through 29. Base your answers on "Jeff's Journal."

24. According to Jeff's journal entry, what do prep cooks need to do BEFORE slicing fruits and vegetables?

    Ⓐ serve the waiting customers
    Ⓑ chop the ingredients
    Ⓒ arrange the desserts
    Ⓓ clean the food

25. What is the main job of a cook on the "hot line"?

    Ⓕ to prepare meat and fish dishes
    Ⓖ to make the food look nice before it is served
    Ⓗ to prepare fancy desserts
    Ⓘ to bake pastries

26. Read this sentence from the story.

    They teach you how to prepare food, cook different dishes, and how to make food appear attractive when it is served.

    What does *dishes* mean in this sentence?

    Ⓐ gives out
    Ⓑ gossips
    Ⓒ plates
    Ⓓ meals

Reading Comprehension   21   **GO ON**

© Harcourt • Grade 4

27. Which BEST describes why Jeff might want to study cooking in another country?

   F to learn more about the cooking in that country

   G to move farther away from his parents

   H to enjoy himself after college

   I to become a lead chef

28. What is the main reason Jeff learned to love to cook?

   A looking forward to being a boss

   B watching shows on television

   C cooking with his parents

   D reading about cooking

29. Based on his journal entry, which BEST describes Jeff?

   F dedicated

   G unsure

   H bossy

   I funny

Read the article "The American Flag" before answering Numbers 30 through 35.

The American Flag

An Early American Flag

Before the end of the war for independence from England, Americans had many different flags. Then the first unofficial American flag appeared. This American flag had the British flag in the upper left-hand corner. The rest of the flag was covered with red and white stripes.

The First Official Flag

When America won its freedom, Americans wanted a new flag. They did not want a flag that looked like Britain's. American leaders met to talk about what the new flag should look like.

On June 14, 1777, Congress passed the first flag resolution. It said that the American flag would have thirteen red and white stripes and that there would be thirteen white stars against a blue background.

No one knows for sure who came up with the idea for how the first American flag should look. Francis Hopkinson, who helped develop government seals, may have helped. Credit sometimes also goes to Betsy Ross, who some believe sewed the first American flag.

After the war, each star and each stripe represented the thirteen colonies. It was decided that the number of stars would change each time a new state joined the union, but the number of stripes would stay the same.

Flag Code Rules

In 1923, leaders met in Washington D.C. to create a set of rules for how to handle the American flag. In 1942, these rules became official. They are known as the Flag Code.

Here are a few of the rules:
- The flag should be raised quickly, but lowered slowly.
- The flag should not be flown in bad weather, unless it is an all-weather flag.
- The flag should never touch the ground.
- The flag should be flown at night only if it is well lighted.

Today's Flag

The flag we have now dates from July 4, 1960, when Hawaii became a state. That increased the number of stars on the flag to 50. Our American flag has a rich history. We can be proud of the Stars and Stripes.

Read about other important events related to the flag throughout history.

Flag Events in History

1777	Continental Congress adopts the following: *Resolved: that the flag of the United States be thirteen stripes, alternate red and white; that the union be thirteen stars, white in a blue field, representing a new constellation.* (The stars represent Delaware, Pennsylvania, New Jersey, Georgia, Connecticut, Massachusetts, Maryland, South Carolina, New Hampshire, Virginia, New York, North Carolina, and Rhode Island.)
1814	Francis Scott Key writes "The Star-Spangled Banner." It officially becomes the national anthem in 1931.
1869	The first flag appears on a postage stamp.
1960	The 50th star is added to the flag as Hawaii becomes a state.
1969	The American flag is placed on the moon by Neil Armstrong.

Name _____

Benchmark Assessment

Beginning-of-Year

▶ Now answer Numbers 30 through 35. Base your answers on the article "The American Flag."

30. What do the stripes on the American flag represent?

    Ⓐ the number of stars on the British flag

    Ⓑ the rules in the Flag Code

    Ⓒ the number of states today

    Ⓓ the original thirteen colonies

31. What happened BEFORE American leaders passed the first flag resolution?

    Ⓕ Congress passed the Flag Code.

    Ⓖ American leaders met to discuss the flag.

    Ⓗ Francis Scott Key wrote "The Star-Spangled Banner."

    Ⓘ Francis Hopkinson helped design the American flag.

32. Read this sentence from the article.

    Francis Hopkinson, who helped develop government seals, may have helped.

    What does the word *seals* mean in this sentence?

    Ⓐ ocean animals

    Ⓑ stamps

    Ⓒ to close

    Ⓓ symbols

Reading Comprehension

GO ON

33. In which section can you find out about the correct handling of the United States Flag?

   Ⓕ An Early American Flag

   Ⓖ The First Official Flag

   Ⓗ Flag Code Rules

   Ⓘ Today's Flag

34. According to the chart, when did "The Star-Spangled Banner" become the national anthem?

   Ⓐ 1814

   Ⓑ 1869

   Ⓒ 1931

   Ⓓ 1969

35. According to the timeline, which of these was a member of the thirteen original colonies?

   Ⓕ Britain

   Ⓖ Hawaii

   Ⓗ Delaware

   Ⓘ Washington

Name _____

Benchmark Assessment

Beginning-of-Year

Vocabulary and Word Analysis

▶ Choose the best word to complete each sentence for Numbers 36 through 45.

36. The girl's mother gave her a _____ hug.
    Ⓐ tender
    Ⓑ brittle
    Ⓒ drowsy
    Ⓓ cunning

37. The elephants at the zoo were _____.
    Ⓕ suggested
    Ⓖ enormous
    Ⓗ grainy
    Ⓘ shallow

38. The student was hurt by the jokes he _____.
    Ⓐ yanked
    Ⓑ overheard
    Ⓒ exclaimed
    Ⓓ conserved

39. The eagle _____ over the trees.
    Ⓕ swoops
    Ⓖ individually
    Ⓗ inhabitants
    Ⓘ plummet

Vocabulary and Word Analysis

GO ON

Name _____

Benchmark Assessment

Beginning-of-Year

40. The bridge may _____ in the wind.
    - (A) occur
    - (B) dreadful
    - (C) sway
    - (D) inevitable

41. Rosa liked to attend _____ events.
    - (F) spiral
    - (G) infinite
    - (H) social
    - (I) aligned

42. Animals that stay awake at night are called _____.
    - (A) ridiculous
    - (B) nocturnal
    - (C) disgraceful
    - (D) contented

43. His parents did not like to see _____ in his room.
    - (F) detail
    - (G) boasting
    - (H) clutter
    - (I) shifting

Vocabulary and Word Analysis

GO ON

Name _____

Benchmark Assessment
Beginning-of-Year

44. The boy knew that having a pet was a big _____.
   - Ⓐ affordable
   - Ⓑ responsibility
   - Ⓒ fondness
   - Ⓓ remark

45. A mirror _____ light.
   - Ⓕ reflects
   - Ⓖ drifts
   - Ⓗ reels
   - Ⓘ rotates

Vocabulary and Word Analysis

Name _____

Benchmark Assessment

Beginning-of-Year

▶ **Choose the best word or words to complete each sentence for Numbers 46 through 51.**

46. The second piano was _____ than the first.
    - Ⓐ loud
    - Ⓑ louder
    - Ⓒ loudest
    - Ⓓ most loud

47. The richest person has _____ money.
    - Ⓕ the least
    - Ⓖ a little
    - Ⓗ the most
    - Ⓘ a bit more

48. The family would often _____ on what to have for dinner.
    - Ⓐ misagree
    - Ⓑ unagree
    - Ⓒ disagree
    - Ⓓ reagree

49. The dancer was famous for her _____ leaps.
    - Ⓕ graceful
    - Ⓖ graceless
    - Ⓗ gracely
    - Ⓘ graceable

Vocabulary and Word Analysis

GO ON

© Harcourt • Grade 4

Name _____

**Benchmark Assessment
Beginning-of-Year**

50. The wet match was _____.
    - Ⓐ useable
    - Ⓑ useous
    - Ⓒ useful
    - Ⓓ useless

51. The kittens cried for _____ food.
    - Ⓕ their
    - Ⓖ they're
    - Ⓗ there
    - Ⓘ they'll

Vocabulary and Word Analysis

Name _____

Benchmark Assessment

Beginning-of-Year

▶ Read and answer Numbers 52 through 55.

52. In which sentence is the underlined word used incorrectly?

    Ⓐ We walked by the park.
    Ⓑ Herbie wanted to buy the hat.
    Ⓒ I went to the school in a hurry.
    Ⓓ The girls had too dollars each.

53. Which word means the SAME as ripe?

    Ⓕ eat
    Ⓖ tear
    Ⓗ ready
    Ⓘ cling

54. Which word means the OPPOSITE of forget?

    Ⓐ transit
    Ⓑ recall
    Ⓒ insult
    Ⓓ persist

55. Which word means the OPPOSITE of dim?

    Ⓕ frail
    Ⓖ bright
    Ⓗ dark
    Ⓘ wet

Vocabulary and Word Analysis

STOP

Name _____

Writing Strategies and Conventions

Benchmark Assessment
Beginning-of-Year

▶ Below is a first draft of a story that Aidan wrote. The story has some mistakes. Read the story to answer Numbers 56 through 58.

Chocolate Melts First

→ [1] Albert was doing his science homework. [2] He had lined up three burners. [3] On each, he was going to heat a different substance. [4] In one he had placed two chocolate candies. [5] In the next he put a wax candle. [6] In the last, he put a metal bolt. [7] He was going to see how long it took each to melt. [8] His homework was to write down the melting time for each. [9] Spelling and geography were Albert's favorite subjects.

→ [10] "Do this with an adult," his teacher had said. [11] "Those burners get hot. [12] This is not safe to do by yourself."

→ [13] So Albert had his mom and dad both helping him. [14] Each of them was watching one of the burners. [15] Each one was holding a clock or a watch.

→ [16] Albert was watching the burner with the chocolate in it. [17] He turned away to get his notebook and pencil. [18] When he turned back, the chocolate was gone. [19] He looked up and saw that his brother had walked into the room.

→ [20] "Thanks for the chocolate," said his brother, happily chewing. [21] "What are you doing?"

→ [22] "A science experiment," said Albert. [23] "And I just learned something. [24] Chocolate melts first."

GO ON

Name _____

Benchmark Assessment

Beginning-of-Year

56. Which transition words should be added to the beginning of sentence 7 to help connect the ideas in the first paragraph?

Ⓐ But

Ⓑ Now

Ⓒ Because

Ⓓ Also

57. Which sentence should be added after sentence 17 to support the ideas in the fourth paragraph?

Ⓕ The students did a science experiment every day.

Ⓖ He needed to be ready to write down the melting times.

Ⓗ Albert was glad when his parents helped him with homework.

Ⓘ Albert had more homework this year than last year.

58. The writer wants to add a new paragraph to the story. Which event below should be added after the last paragraph to keep the story focused on the main idea?

Ⓐ Albert takes a spelling test on science words at school.

Ⓑ Albert and his family eat dinner together.

Ⓒ Albert warns his brother not to eat the candy the next time.

Ⓓ Albert makes a map of the world for geography homework.

Writing Strategies and Conventions

GO ON

Makayla wrote the letter below to her principal. The letter contains mistakes. Read the letter to answer Numbers 59 through 62.

1000 Travis Road
Austin, TX 73301
September 5, 20___

Dear Principal Lopez,

→ ⬚1 I am writing to ask if we can get more computers in our classrooms. ⬚2 In Mr. Schnell's class, we have just one computer. ⬚3 I want to tell you why having student computers in the classroom is so important.

→ ⬚4 First of all, we live in an age of technology. ⬚5 I know we are young, but it is never too early to learn a skill that will be important our whole lives.

→ ⬚6 Second, computers would help us become better students. ⬚7 Writing on a computer makes it easier to revise and edit your writing. ⬚8 When we have a question, a computer would be like having a library in the classroom. ⬚9 Field trips are also a great way for students to learn.

→ ⬚10 You might think that most of us have computers at home. ⬚11 This inequality is part of the problem. ⬚12 Many of us have computers, but some do not. ⬚13 Having student computers in school would make things equal.

→ ⬚14 I know computers are expensive. ⬚15 There must be companies in town that would help pay for computers. ⬚16 We could also have school fundraisers. ⬚17 Our school is a good place to learn. ⬚18 With more computers, you could make it a great place to learn.

Sincerely,
Makayla

Name _____

Benchmark Assessment
Beginning-of-Year

59. Which sentence is off topic and should be taken out of the letter?

   F) sentence 5
   G) sentence 9
   H) sentence 12
   I) sentence 18

60. Which sentence should be added after sentence 4 to support the ideas in the second paragraph?

   A) Most jobs will require that we use a computer.
   B) My brother and I love to play computer games.
   C) Different students learn in different ways.
   D) My teacher suggested that I write to you.

61. Which transition words should be added to the beginning of sentence 8 to help connect the ideas in the paragraph?

   F) Also
   G) On the other hand
   H) Despite this
   I) To sum up

62. The writer wants to add the following sentence to the letter.

   CD-ROM encyclopedias and online resources can be very useful to answer questions and do research.

   Where should this sentence be added to correctly organize the ideas?

   A) after sentence 2
   B) after sentence 5
   C) after sentence 8
   D) after sentence 13

Writing Strategies and Conventions

GO ON

Name _____

Benchmark Assessment

Beginning-of-Year

▶ Below is a first draft of a story that Julia wrote. The story has some mistakes. Read the story to answer Numbers 63 through 65.

The Dance Recital

→ [1] Cho loved to dance, but she hated to perform. [2] She happily went to dance class every week. [3] She also played tennis and piano. [4] She danced around the yard while her parents gardened. [5] She danced around the house when she did her chores. [6] But when it was time for her end-of-year recital, she froze. [7] Each year she took one look at the audience, and ran off the stage.

→ [8] She wanted this year to be different. [9] Her dad had an idea.

→ [10] "You love to dance in the garden," he said. [11] "What if you imagine that the people in the audience are flowers? [12] Picture a field of flowers. [13] It will be just like dancing in the garden."

→ [14] In the weeks before her recital, Cho danced every day. [15] She knew her steps by heart. [16] If she could just stop her nerves, her recital would be perfect.

→ [17] The day of the recital arrived. [18] Cho tried to stay calm. [19] However, by the time she changed into her costume for the show, she was sure she could not perform. [20] She remembered what her dad had said. [21] She walked on the stage, trying to think of flowers. [22] Then she looked out to the audience. [23] Everyone in the audience was holding a flower. [24] The flowers were all from Cho's garden. [25] She saw her mother and father, each smiling at her from behind a flower. [26] Cho smiled, too, and then she began to dance.

Writing Strategies and Conventions 37 **GO ON**

© Harcourt • Grade 4

Name _____

Benchmark Assessment

Beginning-of-Year

63. Which sentence contains a detail that is unimportant to the story?

   Ⓕ sentence 1
   Ⓖ sentence 3
   Ⓗ sentence 10
   Ⓘ sentence 18

64. Which sentence should be added after sentence 5 to support the ideas in the first paragraph?

   Ⓐ She asked her parents for advice to calm her nerves.
   Ⓑ Her best friend, Lottie, loved to perform.
   Ⓒ She danced perfectly when no one was watching her.
   Ⓓ Cho had a picture of herself dancing as a baby.

65. The writer wants to add this sentence to the last paragraph:

   Cho woke up and felt that old nervous feeling in her stomach.

   Where should this sentence be added to keep the events of the story in order?

   Ⓕ after sentence 17
   Ⓖ after sentence 18
   Ⓗ after sentence 19
   Ⓘ after sentence 20

Writing Strategies and Conventions

GO ON

Read the story "Super Brother." Choose the word or words that correctly complete Numbers 66 through 68.

Super Brother

My name is Alex, but you can call me Super Brother. I got the name this morning. My baby brother, Walter, would not stop crying.

First Mom tried to feed him. Walter still cried. Then Grandma tried to __(66)__ rock him. He still cried. Then Dad tried changing his diaper. He cried even louder! Next, Grandpa tried bouncing him on his lap. He still cried.

Finally I __(67)__ to the rescue. I made funny faces. Walter laughed.

I __(68)__ sure what having a baby in the house would be like. I did not know. But now that I am Super Brother, I don't think it will be so bad.

66. Which answer should go in blank (66)?
    - Ⓐ gently
    - Ⓑ gentle
    - Ⓒ gentleness

67. Which answer should go in blank (67)?
    - Ⓕ came
    - Ⓖ will come
    - Ⓗ come

68. Which answer should go in blank (68)?
    - Ⓐ was
    - Ⓑ wasn't
    - Ⓒ wasn't not

Name _____

Benchmark Assessment

Beginning-of-Year

▶ Read the story "The Greek Festival." Choose the word or words that correctly complete Numbers 69 through 71.

The Greek Festival

We go to the Greek Festival in our town every year. It is a family tradition of ours. In the weeks before the festival, if any of us kids __(69)__, my parents say, "Do you want to go to the Greek Festival, or not?" That always gets us back to behaving well!

What is so great about the festival? First of all, they have the __(70)__ delicious Greek food you can get outside of Greece. The Greek dancing __(71)__ fun to watch. And the Greek music even makes me want to dance.

We have never missed the Greek Festival. I hope we never do. I can't wait to go back next year.

69. Which answer should go in blank (69)?
    - Ⓕ misbehave
    - Ⓖ rebehave
    - Ⓗ overbehave

70. Which answer should go in blank (70)?
    - Ⓐ goodest
    - Ⓑ more
    - Ⓒ most

71. Which answer should go in blank (71)?
    - Ⓕ is
    - Ⓖ be
    - Ⓗ was

Writing Strategies and Conventions

GO ON

Name _____

Benchmark Assessment

Beginning-of-Year

▶ **Read and answer Numbers 72 through 75.**

72. In which sentence below is all **capitalization** correct?

　Ⓐ On the first sunday of every month, mrs. martinez visits Friends.

　Ⓑ On the first Sunday of every month, Mrs. Martinez visits friends.

　Ⓒ On the first Sunday of every Month, Mrs. Martinez visits friends.

73. In which sentence below is all **punctuation** correct?

　Ⓕ He was born on Saturday, October 7, 1995

　Ⓖ He was born on Saturday October 7 1995

　Ⓗ He was born on, Saturday October 7 1995

74. Put the ideas in the box together to create a sentence that makes sense.

> to bed
> Dylan brushed
> before he went
> his teeth

Which sentence below correctly combines the words from the box?

　Ⓐ Before he went to bed, his teeth Dylan brushed.

　Ⓑ Dylan brushed his teeth before he went to bed.

　Ⓒ To bed, Dylan brushed his teeth before he went.

Writing Strategies and Conventions

© Harcourt • Grade 4

GO ON

Name _____

Benchmark Assessment

Beginning-of-Year

75. Combine the sentences below to make one sentence.

> Meryl ate a sandwich.
> It was delicious.
> It was made with peanut butter and jelly.

Which sentence correctly combines the sentences in the box?

Ⓕ Meryl ate a sandwich it was delicious peanut butter and jelly.

Ⓖ Meryl ate a delicious peanut butter and jelly sandwich.

Ⓗ Meryl ate a delicious sandwich it was made with peanut butter and jelly.

Writing Strategies and Conventions

GO ON

Name _____

Benchmark Assessment
• • • • • • • • • • •
Beginning-of-Year

▶ For Numbers 76 through 80, read each sentence. Choose the sentence that has the underlined word misspelled. If none of the underlined words are misspelled, choose the answer "No mistake."

76. Ⓐ The seas remained uncharted.
    Ⓑ It is not likely that it will occur.
    Ⓒ The machine generates a lot of heat.
    Ⓓ No mistake

77. Ⓕ The car has ampel room for passengers.
    Ⓖ The reviewer loved the play's futuristic story.
    Ⓗ The crowd stood watching in amazement.
    Ⓘ No mistake

78. Ⓐ Most dogs eagerly wait for their owners to return.
    Ⓑ The grandson was going to inhirit her money.
    Ⓒ We like to collaborate with each other.
    Ⓓ No mistake

79. Ⓕ They watched the fish beneath the surface.
    Ⓖ The lawyer presented his evidance.
    Ⓗ The carousel rotates slowly.
    Ⓘ No mistake

80. Ⓐ The hawk is a bird of prey.
    Ⓑ He was an inventive thinker.
    Ⓗ The cake had an elaborate design.
    Ⓓ No mistake

Writing Strategies and Conventions   43   STOP

Name _____

Benchmark Assessment

Beginning-of-Year

Writing to a Prompt

Everyone has had a special day that he or she will always remember. Think about a special day that you will always remember. Now write a story about that day.

Planning Page

▶ Use this space to make your notes before you begin writing. The writing on this page will NOT be scored.

_____
_____
_____
_____
_____
_____
_____
_____
_____
_____
_____
_____
_____
_____

Writing to a Prompt

GO ON

Name _____

Benchmark Assessment

Beginning-of-Year

▶ **Begin writing here. The writing on this page and the next WILL be scored.**

Writing to a Prompt

45

GO ON

Name _____

Benchmark Assessment

Beginning-of-Year

Writing to a Prompt

Oral Reading Fluency

Have you ever seen a picture of earthworms in a garden? Or, have you seen one near the edge of a sidewalk? They seem so ordinary we hardly think they are worth noticing. However, there are about 3,000 different kinds of these worms. Although we know quite a bit about them, they can still amaze us.

Earthworms belong to a group of worms whose bodies are divided into sections. These sections work together to allow the worm to travel. When you see an earthworm crawling, pay attention to how it moves.

Another special detail about the worm is that it is hard to tell where its head is. You can't tell by looking in its eyes. That is because this worm does not have eyes like people do. The worm can just sense light and dark. The end with the mouth is more pointed than the other end, and that is how you can tell where the head is.

An earthworm's skin must stay wet in order for it to live. If its skin dries out, the worm dies. Therefore, worms prefer damp places, like soil. A worm does not breathe the way you do. It takes in oxygen through its skin.

Perhaps the earthworm is not quite so common after all.

Lynn swam smoothly between the ocean waves. As the water rolled across her shiny, gray back, she glanced over at her mother swimming with a group of her friends a short distance away. Swiftly, pretending she was an arrow, she plunged straight down into the waves, swimming very rapidly. Next she pushed her powerful body straight up into the sky as high as she could. She broke the surface next to her mother with an enormous splash. Her mother splashed her back with a mighty wave of her flipper.

They played in the salty water until a strange sight on the beach caught Lynn's attention. She stopped swimming and stared at two strange, upright creatures who were facing her and pointing. She wondered what they were, and her mother explained to her that those were two human beings. Lynn could see the people waving at her, so she waved back with her great, flexible tail. Mother then suggested to Lynn that they begin the search for lunch. Lynn swam in place beside her mother. She realized that no life could be more wonderful than hers—life as a bottlenose dolphin.

HARCOURT SCHOOL PUBLISHERS
STORYtown

Grade 4

Beginning-of-Year Assessment

Benchmark Assessments

www.harcourtschool.com

Part No. 9997-85845-X (Package of 12)

HARCOURT SCHOOL PUBLISHERS
STORYtown

Grade 4 Benchmark Assessment
Mid-Year

Name _____ Date _____

Performance Summary

                                             Student Score

READING

Reading Comprehension
- Multiple-Choice Items   _____/32
- Short-Response Open-Ended Item   _____/2
- Short-Response Open-Ended Item   _____/2
- Extended-Response Open-Ended Item   _____/4

Vocabulary and Word Analysis   _____/20

Total Student Reading Score   _____/60

WRITING
- Writing Strategies and Conventions   _____/25
- Writing Prompt   _____/6

ORAL READING FLUENCY
- Passage 1   _____ Words Correct Per Minute
- Passage 2   _____ Words Correct Per Minute

(Bubble in the appropriate performance level.)

Reading

Below Basic	Basic (On-Level)	Proficient (On-Level)	Advanced
1–35	36–45	46–55	56–60
○	○	○	○

Writing Conventions

Below Basic	Basic (On-Level)	Proficient (On-Level)	Advanced
1–10	11–15	16–19	20–25
○	○	○	○

Writing Prompt

Below Basic	Basic (On-Level)	Proficient (On-Level)	Advanced
1–2	3–4	5	6
○	○	○	○

Oral Reading Fluency

25th Percentile	50th Percentile	75th Percentile	90th Percentile
87 WCPM	112 WCPM	139 WCPM	166 WCPM
○	○	○	○

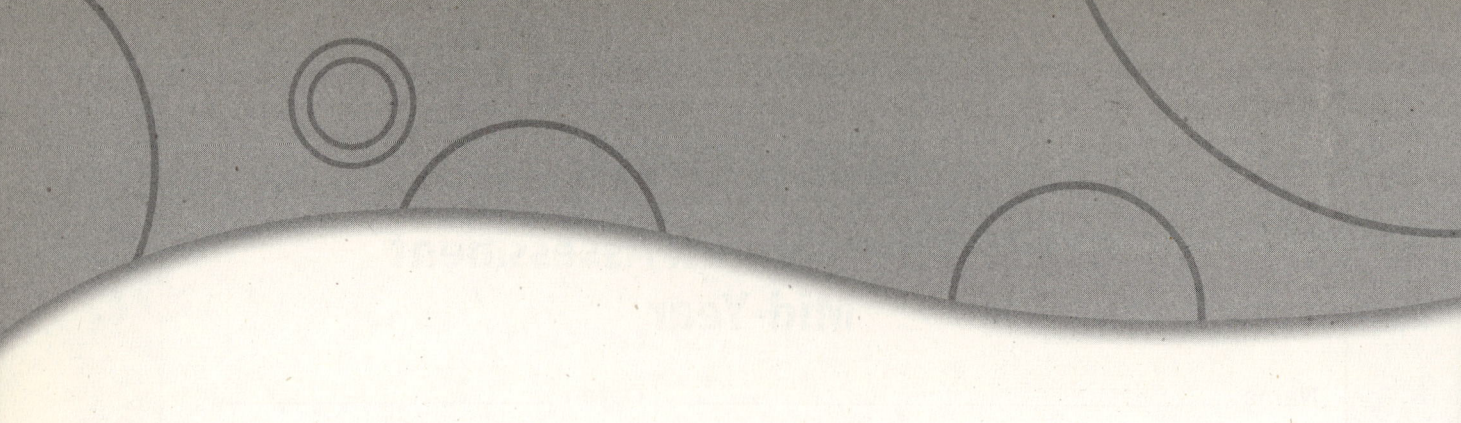

For permission to reprint copyrighted material, grateful acknowledgment is made to the following sources:

Carus Publishing Company, 30 Grove St., Suite C, Peterborough, NH 03458: "Digging for Africa's Lost Dinosaurs" by Lesley Reed from *APPLESEEDS: Digging Up Dinosaurs*, January 2005. Text copyright © 2005 by Carus Publishing Company.

Highlights for Children, Inc., Columbus, Ohio: "A Tree Needs a Special Place" by Lyda Williamson, illustrated by Laura Jacobsen from *Highlights for Children* Magazine, April 2005. Copyright © 2005 by Highlights for Children, Inc.

Copyright © by Harcourt, Inc.

All rights reserved. No part of this publication may be reproduced or transmitted in any form or by any means, electronic or mechanical, including photocopy, recording, or any information storage and retrieval system, without permission in writing from the publisher.

Permission is hereby granted to individuals using the corresponding student's textbook or kit as the major vehicle for regular classroom instruction to photocopy entire pages from this publication in classroom quantities for instructional use and not for resale. Requests for information on other matters regarding duplication of this work should be addressed to School Permissions and Copyrights, Harcourt, Inc., 6277 Sea Harbor Drive, Orlando, Florida 32887-6777. Fax: 407-345-2418.

HARCOURT and the Harcourt Logo are trademarks of Harcourt, Inc., registered in the United States of America and/or other jurisdictions.

Printed in the United States of America

ISBN 10 0-15-358768-7   ISBN 13 978-0-15-358768-9

1 2 3 4 5 6 7 8 9 10   073   16 15 14 13 12 11 10 09 08 07

If you have received these materials as examination copies free of charge, Harcourt School Publishers retains title to the materials and they may not be resold. Resale of examination copies is strictly prohibited and is illegal.

Possession of this publication in print format does not entitle users to convert this publication, or any portion of it, into electronic format.

Read the article "Digging for Africa's Lost Dinosaurs" before answering Numbers 1 through 6.

Digging For Africa's Lost Dinosaurs
By Lesley Reed

"Paleontology is more than science," says world-famous paleontologist Paul Sereno. "You get to travel, meet new people, and have adventures." He should know—he's spent 15 years on one of the greatest dinosaur adventures ever.

For millions of years, dinosaur fossils have lain untouched in Africa's Sahara desert—that is, until Sereno decided to brave the extreme heat and harsh travel. Before Sereno went to Africa, very few dinosaurs had been discovered on that continent. Sereno knew that the secret to finding lots of new fossils was to go where no one else had gone. But crossing the Sahara to search for fossils was not going to be easy.

On Sereno's first expedition, he and his team crossed 1,500 miles of desert. They climbed over sand dunes the size of mountains. When they arrived in the country of Niger, the government wouldn't allow them to dig. And robbers were such a problem that the team needed an armed guard. After working everything out, they had only a short time to do their work. But they discovered a dinosaur gold mine. Sereno and his team found one of the richest dinosaur "beds" in Africa.

Within days, they found the remains of a new meat-eating dinosaur. Bigger and faster than Allosaurus, they named it *Afrovenator*, for "African hunter." They found and named many others. *Suchomimus* had a sail on its back and a long crocodile-like snout used for catching fish. (The Sahara once had a lot of water.)

Nigersauras had 600 teeth. And *Sarcosuchus* was a crocodile-like dinosaur as long as a bus.

Workers and others crowd around the skeleton of a *Suchomimus*, which may have been 36 feet long and 12 feet high.

There are many challenges to working in the Sahara. With temperatures over 120 degrees, it's easy to feel like a cookie baking in an oven. Fortunately, Sereno doesn't mind. "I adapt to heat like a lizard," he says. And he drinks lots of water.

Where does he get water in the desert? He and his team carry it with them. From medical supplies to freeze-dried ice cream bars, the team takes whatever they need. On one trip, they carried 600 pounds of pasta and 4,000 gallons of water.

Measuring the length of a *Sarcosuchus*, the "Super Croc," which was about 40 feet long.

All the effort is worth it. "Every dinosaur we've found in Africa is new," says Sereno. "Not one is the same as those on other continents. That's why it's thrilling—it's a lost world."

Paul Sereno discovering the thighbone of the *Jobaria*, a dinosaur that weighed about 20 tons.

Name _____

Benchmark Assessment
Mid-Year

▶ Now answer Numbers 1 through 6. Base your answers on the article "Digging for Africa's Lost Dinosaurs."

1. Read these sentences from the article.

   > "Paleontology is more than science," says world-famous paleontologist Paul Sereno. "You get to travel, meet new people, and have adventures." He should know—he's spent 15 years on one of the greatest dinosaur adventures ever.

   What does the suffix *-ologist* in the word *paleontologist* suggest the word means?

   Ⓐ one who studies
   Ⓑ one who experiences life
   Ⓒ one who believes in science
   Ⓓ one who travels the world

2. Why were few dinosaur fossils discovered in Africa's Sahara desert for millions of years?

   Ⓕ The heat had destroyed most fossils.
   Ⓖ Not many dinosaurs had lived in Africa.
   Ⓗ The area is a difficult place to travel in and dig.
   Ⓘ The area was protected by armed guards.

3. Why does Sereno need armed guards for his digs?

   Ⓐ His digs are against the law.
   Ⓑ There are problems with robbers.
   Ⓒ The Sahara is crowded with people.
   Ⓓ There is a threat of wild animals.

Reading Comprehension

GO ON

Name _____

4. What happens right AFTER Sereno and his team find their first dinosaur bed in Africa?
   - F They have to climb over sand dunes that are the size of mountains.
   - G They learn the government of Niger will not let them dig.
   - H They find the remains of a new meat-eating dinosaur.
   - I They discover a dinosaur that had a sail on its back.

5. Why does the author say that Sereno's team found a dinosaur "gold mine"?
   - A The fossils had been buried with treasures.
   - B The team had to dig very deep for what they found.
   - C The fossils they found were numerous.
   - D The team risked being trapped inside their digs.

6. How does the article say that the Sahara desert today is DIFFERENT than it used to be millions of years ago?
   - F Today it is hot and dry, but it used to have a lot of water.
   - G Today it is home to dinosaurs, but it never was before.
   - H It once was an easy place to search, but not anymore.
   - I It once had mountains, but now it is flat.

Name _____

▶ Read the story "Being a Good Friend" before answering Numbers 7 through 13.

Benchmark Assessment
Mid-Year

Being a Good Friend

Ellie hummed to herself as she waited for Jada at their usual meeting place, the oak tree by the traffic light. The two classmates had been best friends since they were introduced to each other in kindergarten. They met at that spot almost every day after school was dismissed, and then, laughing and chatting, they accompanied each other for the walk home.

Ellie's apartment building was the first stop. The girls would arrive there, have some refreshments, and stay for awhile to play and to visit.

As Ellie waited this afternoon, she scanned the lawn for four-leaf clovers that she could give to Jada, because Jada considered them a sign of good luck.

Ellie was concentrating so hard on her search that she didn't notice Jada had passed by. When she looked up, she saw Jada walking with Katie, whose family had just moved there from out of state.

Ellie scrambled to her feet and reached for her knapsack. She called out to Jada, but her friend acted as if she had not heard. Ellie raced down the street until she caught up with Jada.

"Hey, did you forget about me?" Ellie asked.

Jada and Katie exchanged glances. Then Jada looked coolly at Ellie.

"I thought I saw you sitting there, but I wasn't sure," she said.

"Why didn't you say anything?"

"You were so busy picking at the grass, I didn't want to disturb you," Jada said.

Her new friend giggled, and made no effort to hide her amusement. Ellie felt embarrassed and confused at the idea of Jada making fun of her. She turned away abruptly and walked to her house alone. After closing the door behind her, she peered out the window as the two girls walked together past her house.

The next day, Ellie wondered if Jada would call for her on her way to school. However, when she saw Jada approaching with her new friend, Ellie hid in the living room until they were out of sight. Later she trudged to school by herself, feeling more alone than she had ever felt in her life.

After the dismissal bell sounded, Ellie waited again by the oak tree. This time, she didn't search for clovers. Instead, she pretended to be fascinated by her math textbook. When she heard giggling, she knew that Jada and her new friend were nearby. Again, Jada did not stop to give a greeting, so Ellie continued to read as if there were nothing else in the world except that textbook. Inside, however, she felt very sad.

As the days passed, Ellie no longer waited for Jada after school by the oak tree. Ellie missed her friend, but she didn't know how to attract her attention, so she decided to just leave it alone.

One Friday, Ellie noticed Jada leaning up against the bark of the oak tree. She walked over and said hello. Jada smiled shyly.

"I've been such a bad friend," said Jada regretfully. "I'm sorry."

"It's okay," answered Ellie, though the expression on her face showed that it really wasn't.

"It was interesting to meet Katie," Jada went on. "We have a lot of the same interests, you know. But I know that was no excuse to treat you poorly. Now Katie has found a new friend, and I think I know just how you felt. Ellie, can you forgive me?"

When Ellie said yes this time, she meant it sincerely.

"I have something for you," said Jada. She displayed a four-leaf clover, which she had carefully glued to a hand-painted cardboard rectangle. Plastic wrap protected the leaves.

"I found it yesterday in my front yard," Jada went on. "I know it's good luck, since you are still my friend!"

Name _____

Benchmark Assessment
Mid-Year

▶ **Now answer Numbers 7 through 13. Base your answers on the story "Being a Good Friend."**

7. Where does this story first take place?
   - Ⓐ on a neighborhood street
   - Ⓑ in Ellie's living room
   - Ⓒ at the bus stop
   - Ⓓ in Jada's front yard

8. Read these sentences from the story.

   "I've been such a bad friend," said Jada regretfully. "I'm sorry."

   What does *regretfully* mean in the sentence?
   - Ⓕ with a lack of awareness
   - Ⓖ with deep anger over someone else's actions
   - Ⓗ with great confidence in oneself
   - Ⓘ with a sense of sadness or disappointment

9. Why does Jada refuse to answer when Ellie calls to her?
   - Ⓐ She is too interested in her math textbook.
   - Ⓑ She has been trying to hide from Ellie.
   - Ⓒ She does not realize Ellie is there.
   - Ⓓ She is with Katie and ignoring Ellie.

10. Which event helps Jada realize how poorly she has treated Ellie?
    - Ⓕ Ellie's family moves to another state.
    - Ⓖ Ellie tells her how hurt she is.
    - Ⓗ Katie treats Jada the same way.
    - Ⓘ Katie tells Jada she has been mean to Ellie.

Reading Comprehension

GO ON

Name _____

Benchmark Assessment
Mid-Year

11. What does Jada give Ellie at the end of the story?

    Ⓐ a painting she had made

    Ⓑ her math textbook

    Ⓒ a four-leaf clover

    Ⓓ a snack they had once enjoyed together

12. Which BEST describes the theme of the story?

    Ⓕ A good friend would never do anything bad to you.

    Ⓖ It is best to not expect much from your friends so you don't get hurt.

    Ⓗ It is too hard for anyone to be a good friend all of the time.

    Ⓘ A good friend knows when he or she is being a bad friend.

---

13. How is the conflict in this story resolved? Use details and information from the story to support your answer.

    READ THINK EXPLAIN

    _____
    _____
    _____
    _____
    _____
    _____
    _____

Reading Comprehension

GO ON

Name _____

▶ Read the article "Good Health" before answering Numbers 14 through 19.

Benchmark Assessment
Mid-Year

Good Health

What's so great about exercise? Even if the thought of jogging around a track, jumping rope, or getting hot and dirty makes you shudder, there are ways that working out can still be fun. You might enjoy a game like volleyball, or maybe you ride your bicycle with friends. You could also get moving through the daily responsibility of walking your dog.

These are all ways to work out, or exercise. Exercise is a must in order to gain and preserve good health. It strengthens your body, gives you more energy, and even makes you feel happier.

When you exercise, you use your muscles. This makes them stronger, including muscles deep inside the body, such as your heart. The job of the heart muscle is to pump blood throughout the body. The blood contains oxygen, which reaches every part of the body by coursing through blood vessels. A strong heart gets the job done more effectively, and with less effort. It certainly is worthwhile to strengthen that muscle.

When you are healthy, you feel like you have more energy. Energy is the power to move around. A healthy body does not have to work as hard to move, and it does not get tired as quickly.

Another plus about exercise is that is makes you feel good. Exercise causes the body to produce a kind of chemical in the brain that calms you, and raises your spirits too. This chemical change is in addition to the good feelings you get from being stronger and having more energy.

Eating right is another way to stay healthy. Breakfast is very important if you make it a healthy one. It provides power to your body and to your brain.

It's easier to choose healthy foods if you know what you need. Children generally need about a cup and a half of fruit and a cup and a half of vegetables every day. You should drink between four and eight glasses of water and juice each day.

Name _____

Benchmark Assessment
Mid-Year

The final ingredient for good health is to get enough rest. Growing children need an average of nine hours of sleep every night. When the body is asleep it repairs itself.

The body is like a machine. If you take good care of it, it can work well for a long time.

Name _____

Benchmark Assessment

Mid-Year

▶ **Now answer Numbers 14 through 19. Base your answers on the article "Good Health."**

14. What is the article MOSTLY about?
    - Ⓐ what happens to an unhealthy body
    - Ⓑ different ways to have a healthy body
    - Ⓒ what children should eat and drink
    - Ⓓ the importance of exercise

15. Read this sentence from the article.

    The blood contains oxygen, which reaches every part of the body by coursing through blood vessels.

    What does *coursing* mean in this sentence?
    - Ⓕ filtering out
    - Ⓖ dripping into
    - Ⓗ carrying back
    - Ⓘ passing through

16. How does sleep help the body?
    - Ⓐ gives it more oxygen
    - Ⓑ allows it to repair itself
    - Ⓒ raises its spirits
    - Ⓓ pumps blood through it

Reading Comprehension

GO ON

© Harcourt • Grade 4

Name _____

17. Why does the author say that the body is "like a machine"?

　　Ⓕ It is very powerful.

　　Ⓖ It works all the time.

　　Ⓗ To get it to work well, you must take good care of it.

　　Ⓘ It does what you need it to do automatically, with no effort from you.

18. How is a healthy body DIFFERENT from an unhealthy body?

　　Ⓐ The healthy body has more energy.

　　Ⓑ The healthy body has less energy.

　　Ⓒ The healthy body never gets tired.

　　Ⓓ The healthy body gets tired quickly.

Reading Comprehension

Name _____

Benchmark Assessment
Mid-Year

19. According to the article, what are the effects of exercise? Use details and information from the article to explain your answer.

READ
THINK
EXPLAIN

_____
_____
_____
_____
_____
_____
_____
_____
_____
_____
_____
_____
_____
_____

Read the story "A Tree Needs a Special Place" before answering Numbers 20 through 25.

A Tree Needs a Special Place

by Lyda Williamson
illustrated by Laura Jacobsen

Oscar leaped up onto the porch and bounded into the house. He unzipped his backpack, pulled out a plastic bag, and ran to find *Mamá*.

"Mamá, look!" shouted Oscar. He opened the bag to reveal a baby tree, roots and all. "We got them at school for Arbor Day."

"How exciting!" said Mamá.

Oscar looked at the tree. "But I don't know where to plant it."

Mamá smiled. "It needs a special place. When we moved here from Mexico, I was a little girl. I didn't have any friends. Our new house had a big backyard with an oak tree. My father hung a swing from it, and I'd swing for hours. One day, a little girl came over and asked if she could swing with me. It was Claudia."

Oscar nodded. Claudia was Mamá's best friend. "Maybe someday this tree will grow big enough for a swing," he said. "I'll go show *Abuelito* and *Abuelita*!"

Oscar sprinted downstairs to his grandparents' apartment.

Abuelito, Oscar's grandfather, opened the door. "¡*Hola*, Oscar!"

"Look, Abuelito! I got a tree at school for Arbor Day," Oscar said. "But I don't know where to plant it. We don't have a big backyard like Mamá did."

Abuelito smoothed back his graying hair. "No, but we'll find a place for it," he said. He squatted down to look at the tree. "Back in Mexico, the sun is so strong at midday that everyone must take a break. A huge paloverde tree grew at the edge of our cornfield. I loved to rest in its shade."

Abuelita laughed. "I can still picture you there!" She put her hand on Oscar's shoulder. "Let me tell you about my favorite trees," she said. "My mamá loved to make *agua de limón*. It's like lemonade, but it's made with limes. Lime trees grew everywhere in my town! Mamá would send me out to pick the limes, then she'd let me stir the water, juice, and sugar. We'd use colorful straws to sip our cool green drinks."

"Mmmm, sounds good," said Oscar.

"I'll make it for you sometime," said Abuelita. "Now go find a spot to plant *your* tree."

"I will!" said Oscar. He raced up the steps and out the front door. Just as he stepped onto the porch, *Papá* pulled up in his car.

"What do you have there?" asked Papá.

Oscar showed him the tree.

Papá smiled. "When I was a boy in Michigan, my father would always make guacamole with avocados from the store."

Oscar nodded. He liked the tasty green dip.

"He'd mix it up and talk about Mexico. One time he saved the avocado seed. We put it in water. Every day, I watched it. Soon a tiny green sprout appeared. It became a baby tree. We nursed it along, then planted it in the ground."

"Did avocados grow on it, Papá?" asked Oscar.

"No, it couldn't survive the cold winter," Papa said. "But I'll always remember that special time with my father."

Oscar's sister walked up the sidewalk toward them.

"Magdalena, look!" Oscar held up the tree. "But I need a place to plant it."

"Let's see," said Magdalena. "At our old house, when you were a baby, a huge poplar tree grew near our sidewalk. It was taller than every other tree around. Wherever I was in town, I could always see our tree high above everything else."

Oscar glanced at the wide strip of grass between their sidewalk and the street. It was the perfect place! "Thanks, Magdalena—I'm going to plant my tree right here."

The sun was beginning to set. By now, the rest of Oscar's family had come outside to see where Oscar would plant his tree.

Oscar read the planting directions. "'Every fall this sugar maple will turn a brilliant red-orange. To plant it, dig a hole twice the size of the roots. Place the roots in the hole, and fill it with dirt. Water the tree often for the first year.'"

Abuelito got the shovel. Mamá got the watering can.

"Ready, Oscar?" asked Papá.

"I'm ready!" Oscar looked around at his family and grinned. "We'll have a beautiful tree right in front of our house for all of us to enjoy."

Papá dug a hole. Oscar held the tree in place as Magdalena, Abuelita, and Abuelito gently pushed dirt around it. When they were finished, Mamá sprinkled water on top.

Everyone stood back to admire the new tree. Oscar couldn't wait to watch it grow.

Name _____

Benchmark Assessment
Mid-Year

▶ Now answer Numbers 20 through 25. Base your answers on the story "A Tree Needs a Special Place."

20. Read this sentence from the story.

> Oscar leaped up onto the porch and bounded into the house.

Which word means about the SAME as *bounded* in this sentence?

- F) hid
- G) strolled
- H) bounced
- I) trembled

21. What is Oscar's problem with his tree?
- A) He thinks it is too small to survive.
- B) He cannot read the directions for planting.
- C) He is unsure where to plant it.
- D) He fears his family will not want it.

22. What happens BEFORE Oscar hears his family's stories about their special trees?
- F) He gets his own tree from school.
- G) He plants his tree with his family.
- H) He decides where to plant his tree.
- I) He reads the directions for planting.

Reading Comprehension

18

GO ON

© Harcourt • Grade 4

Name _____

Benchmark Assessment
Mid-Year

23. What had happened to Mamá because of the tree in her yard?
    Ⓐ She had enjoyed agua de limón.
    Ⓑ She had learned how to be alone and rest.
    Ⓒ She had met her best friend.
    Ⓓ She had spent a lot of time with her father.

24. How is the tree that Papá describes DIFFERENT from the ones Oscar's other family members describe?
    Ⓕ Papá's tree produces fruit, but the others' trees do not.
    Ⓖ Papá's tree does not live long, but the others' trees are fully grown.
    Ⓗ Papá's tree grows in their backyard, but the others' trees grow in other places.
    Ⓘ Papá's tree is enjoyed just by him, but the others' trees are enjoyed by many.

25. Where does Oscar plant his tree?
    Ⓐ next to the sidewalk
    Ⓑ on the other side of town
    Ⓒ in their backyard
    Ⓓ at the edge of a cornfield

Reading Comprehension

GO ON

Read "Ben Liang's Story" before answering Numbers 26 through 29.

Ben Liang's Story

Ben Liang slumped over at his desk in school and stared dejectedly at a blank piece of paper in front of him, worrying about his latest homework assignment. His teacher, Ms. Valdez, had just said to the class, "For the past couple of weeks, we have been reading stories about family, adventures, and pets. Today I want each of you to compose a story about your family, an adventure, or a pet." Ben's spirits plummeted. He had no idea what to write about, and he contemplated his story's topic as he gazed at the sheet of white paper.

Ben and his family had immigrated to America from China when he was still a toddler. His father and mother purchased a small Chinese restaurant, and the apartment upstairs became home to Ben, his father and mother, his grandmother, and his younger sister, Emily. Before he began attending his new school, Ben enjoyed helping his mother and grandmother fold dumplings for their customers. While they prepared the food, they would practice speaking English together. Ben thought that this cherished time with his family might make a good story.

Or Ben could write about feasting on *dim sum*, his favorite Chinese meal, every week with his family and friends. In Chinese, *dim sum* means "a little bit of the heart." Ben thought that was an excellent name because the variety of foods on the *dim sum* table (Chinese dumplings, extraordinary meat dishes, and lots of fresh, hot vegetables) is made from the heart.

On *dim sum* days, Ben and his cousins scampered and played among the empty tables in his parents' restaurant before the customers arrived. One morning, the children quietly opened the kitchen door to watch the cooks making *dim sum*. Suddenly one cook collided with a cart full of food, everything went crashing to the floor, and everyone went running to the kitchen to help. Ben and his relatives labored hard all that day to make more food. Ben smiled as he recalled the *dim sum* incident and thought that perhaps Ms. Valdez would enjoy reading that story.

Then Ben remembered one special Sunday when his father took him along with his mother, sister, and grandmother to a nearby park for a day of relaxation. In the center of the park was a big lake surrounded by tall, green pine trees. Ben's father rented a rowboat and took Ben and Emily out on the lake.

Ben heard his mother shout, "Look, turtles!" She pointed, and Ben's father started rowing in that direction. There, near the bank of the lake, they spotted, dozens of turtles.

"Let's catch one," Ben's father suggested, and Ben and Emily nodded eagerly. As Ben's father rowed nearer to the swimming creatures, Ben reached over the side of the boat to seize one of the biggest turtles.

"I got it!" he yelled as he scooped the turtle into the boat.

"He's huge," giggled Emily. She turned to her father and asked, "Can we keep him?"

Ben's father laughed. "Sure we can," he said. "We can put him in the wading pool I bought for you and Ben a couple of years ago. You will have to be responsible, take very good care of him, and think of a name for him."

What an adventure that had been! Ben smiled to himself, thinking that he still had that turtle, and it was the greatest pet he'd ever owned. He had named his turtle Dim Sum because he thought his pet was a "bit of the heart," just like his favorite family meal.

Ben eventually began to relax as he started writing his assignment for Ms. Valdez. The title of his story would be "Dim Sum: My Pet Turtle."

Name _____

Benchmark Assessment Mid-Year

▶ Now answer Numbers 26 through 29. Base your answers on the article "Ben Liang's Story."

26. Why is Ben unhappy at the beginning of the story?
    - Ⓕ He does not like sitting at his desk.
    - Ⓖ His teacher is boring him.
    - Ⓗ He does not know what to write about.
    - Ⓘ His father purchases a Chinese restaurant.

27. Why is going to the lake important to the story?
    - Ⓐ The lake is full of turtles.
    - Ⓑ It is a special Sunday for Ben's family.
    - Ⓒ Ben gets an idea for his story at the lake.
    - Ⓓ The family eats *dim sum* at the lake.

28. Which sentence from the story is a FACT and not an opinion?
    - Ⓕ "In Chinese, *dim sum* means 'a little bit of the heart.'"
    - Ⓖ "Ben thought that was an excellent name because the variety of foods on the *dim sum* table is made from the heart."
    - Ⓗ "He's huge," giggled Emily."
    - Ⓘ "Ben smiled to himself, thinking that he still had that turtle, and it was the greatest pet he'd ever owned."

29. How will Ben MOST LIKELY feel when he is finished with his story?
    - Ⓐ strange
    - Ⓑ proud
    - Ⓒ comical
    - Ⓓ ordinary

Reading Comprehension

GO ON

Read the article "All About Robots" before answering Numbers 30 through 35.

All About Robots

Did you know that you have robots in your home? Every time an alarm clock rings, you are hearing a robot. When your mother puts food in the microwave, she is using a robot. When you put a movie in to watch, you are using a robot. Robots have many uses.

What is a robot? A robot is a machine that can do work that is normally done by people. The robot is run by a computer, which acts as its "brain." The brain tells the robot what to do.

Robots do many jobs that people do not want to do. They build cars, make parts for machines, and even make candy bars. Many companies use robots because they never get sick, they do not need to eat, and they never have to rest.

Some robots do jobs that are not safe for people to do. For example, the planet Mars would be a dangerous place to visit. So scientists sent robots, instead of people, to check out Mars. The robots gathered important information about Mars. They then relayed that information back to Earth. This helps everyone to know more about the red planet.

Robots can go other places that would not be safe for people. They can go into burning buildings and help put out fires. Scientists use robots to go inside volcanoes and study what is happening. Robots can also be used to learn about the ocean, because they can dive far deeper than people. They gather information about fish and plants that people have never seen before.

Soon robots may be used for even more important jobs. They could help police, doctors, farmers, and families.

Reading Comprehension

Yes, there may be even more robots in your home. Robots to help you clean the house and even to make you lemonade!

Look at the chart to learn about some of the early advances in robot history.

Early Advances in Robotics

Year	Inventor	Nationality	Invention(s)
350 B.C.	Archytas	Greek	Mechanical bird
~200 B.C.	Ctesibus	Greek	Water clocks
1495	Leonardo DaVinci	Italian	Knight in armor
1738	Jacques de Vaucanson	French	Two musical players and a duck
1770	Pierre and Henri-Louis Jaquet-Droz	Swiss	Three dolls

Name _____

Benchmark Assessment
Mid-Year

▶ Now answer Numbers 30 through 35. Base your answers on the article "All About Robots."

30. What does the author use to introduce the definition of "robot"?
    - Ⓕ a question
    - Ⓖ an exclamation
    - Ⓗ underlining
    - Ⓘ italics

31. Read this sentence from the article:

    "The brain tells the robot what to do."

    What does *brain* mean in this sentence?
    - Ⓐ the front part of the head
    - Ⓑ a person who is very intelligent
    - Ⓒ the device to control functions
    - Ⓓ a person who is a good planner

32. According to information in the article, what is MOST LIKELY true about the future of robots?
    - Ⓕ Inventors will learn from their mistakes.
    - Ⓖ Inventors will continue to make better robots.
    - Ⓗ Inventors will start learning more from the past.
    - Ⓘ Inventors will stop sending robots to places that are unsafe.

33. In which column of the chart would you look to find out which inventor was Italian?
    - Ⓐ Year
    - Ⓑ Inventor
    - Ⓒ Nationality
    - Ⓓ Invention(s)

Reading Comprehension

GO ON

Name _____

Benchmark Assessment
Mid-Year

34. According to the chart, how are Archytas and Ctesibus ALIKE?

   Ⓕ Both made inventions in the same year.
   Ⓖ Both have the same last name.
   Ⓗ Both invented something musical.
   Ⓘ Both shared the same nationality.

35. Why did the author write this article? Use details and information from the article to support your answer.

   _____
   _____
   _____
   _____
   _____
   _____
   _____

Reading Comprehension　26　**STOP**

Name _____

Benchmark Assessment · · · · · · · · · · · **Mid-Year**

Vocabulary and Word Analysis

▶ For Numbers 36 through 49, choose the word that best completes each sentence.

36. The people at the fair were _____ by the bugs.
    - Ⓐ muttered
    - Ⓑ flinched
    - Ⓒ craned
    - Ⓓ annoyed

37. The adventures of the sea captain were _____.
    - Ⓕ darted
    - Ⓖ jostling
    - Ⓗ legendary
    - Ⓘ swerved

38. The grapes grow in _____.
    - Ⓐ clusters
    - Ⓑ fury
    - Ⓒ eruption
    - Ⓓ taut

39. The rocking boat made the crew feel _____.
    - Ⓕ constant
    - Ⓖ predators
    - Ⓗ particular
    - Ⓘ queasy

Vocabulary and Word Analysis

GO ON

Name _____

Benchmark Assessment
Mid-Year

40. The teacher asked all students to be _____.
    (A) contradicting
    (B) attentive
    (C) dashed
    (D) immediate

41. The glass vase was very _____.
    (F) delicate
    (G) rumpled
    (H) glared
    (I) flexible

42. The parrot could _____ any voice.
    (A) contract
    (B) lure
    (C) traits
    (D) mimic

43. The factory worker was tired of her job's _____.
    (F) stern
    (G) peculiar
    (H) drudgery
    (I) hermit

44. The runners _____ to the finish line.
    (A) dashed
    (B) gaped
    (C) averted
    (D) discouraged

Vocabulary and Word Analysis

GO ON

Name _____

45. We walked _____ to the funeral.
- Ⓕ sparkling
- Ⓖ treacherous
- Ⓗ stroll
- Ⓘ solemnly

46. We lost the game because of the goalie's _____.
- Ⓐ unstep
- Ⓑ disstep
- Ⓒ prestep
- Ⓓ misstep

47. The teacher asked the student to _____ the test.
- Ⓕ retake
- Ⓖ pretake
- Ⓗ untake
- Ⓘ mistake

48. I liked the shirt that had some _____.
- Ⓐ decoration
- Ⓑ decorate
- Ⓒ decorates
- Ⓓ decorating

49. The friends were _____ to each other.
- Ⓕ devotion
- Ⓖ devote
- Ⓗ devoted
- Ⓘ devotes

Vocabulary and Word Analysis

Name _____

Benchmark Assessment
Mid-Year

▶ **Read and answer Numbers 50 through 55.**

50. Which word means the SAME as remarkable?
    - Ⓐ natural
    - Ⓑ grouchy
    - Ⓒ outstanding
    - Ⓓ sensible

51. Which word means the SAME as understand?
    - Ⓕ feel
    - Ⓖ know
    - Ⓗ like
    - Ⓘ confuse

52. Which word means the OPPOSITE of grief?
    - Ⓐ pain
    - Ⓑ deny
    - Ⓒ need
    - Ⓓ joy

53. Which word means the OPPOSITE of revenge?
    - Ⓕ remain
    - Ⓖ enjoy
    - Ⓗ forgive
    - Ⓘ pretend

Vocabulary and Word Analysis

GO ON

54. In which sentence is the underlined word used incorrectly?

    (A) He boarded the train to the city.
    (B) The cook used two much salt.
    (C) Many leave today for vacation.
    (D) We are leaving in four days.

55. In which sentence is the underlined word used incorrectly?

    (F) We were told to stand over there.
    (G) She put the pretty pink flour in her basket.
    (H) The hunter chased the hare across the field.
    (I) The ball went right into the hole.

Vocabulary and Word Analysis

Name _____

Writing Strategies and Conventions

Benchmark Assessment Mid-Year

▶ Below is a first draft of a story that Jamal wrote. The story has some mistakes. Read the story to answer Numbers 56 through 58.

Picking a Book

→ ⟨1⟩ Tim opened the door to the bookstore. ⟨2⟩ He and his mother walked inside. ⟨3⟩ His mother had promised him a new book to read on their trip this summer.

→ ⟨4⟩ Tim was sure he wanted a book on airplanes. ⟨5⟩ He would be flying on a plane for the first time ever. ⟨6⟩ He wanted to know how planes worked. ⟨7⟩ Tim and his mom lived close to his school.

→ ⟨8⟩ Tim's mom helped him find three books. ⟨9⟩ They were all interesting to Tim especially the one with colorful pictures and diagrams. ⟨10⟩ On the shelf below, however, was a book about cars. ⟨11⟩ Tim had always liked cars. ⟨12⟩ Maybe this book was a better choice.

→ ⟨13⟩ As Tim flipped through pages showing the many kinds of cars built in the last century, his mother moved to the next section of the store. ⟨14⟩ When she returned, she found Tim on the floor. ⟨15⟩ Stacks of books surrounded him. ⟨16⟩ Some were about planes. ⟨17⟩ Others were about cars. ⟨18⟩ Two books were about all kinds of things with engines.

→ ⟨19⟩ Mom held up a new book for Tim to see. ⟨20⟩ Tim saw the cover and smiled. ⟨21⟩ It was a collection of stories about pirates, buried treasure and journeys across the ocean. ⟨22⟩ What Tim really wanted to read during his own travels were exciting tales about adventures long ago.

Writing Strategies and Conventions

© Harcourt • Grade 4

GO ON

56. The writer wants to add the following sentence to the story.

> **During their trip they would also be taking a long car ride to the beach.**

Where should this sentence be added to keep the events of the story in order?

Ⓐ after sentence 8
Ⓑ after sentence 11
Ⓒ after sentence 14
Ⓓ after sentence 22

57. Which sentence below should be added after sentence 21 to support the ideas in the fifth paragraph?

Ⓕ Tim's mother said the book was too much money.
Ⓖ Tim had never really liked either planes or cars.
Ⓗ Tim's mother decided they should go on the trip.
Ⓘ Tim changed his mind about the book he wanted.

58. Which sentence contains a detail that is unimportant to the story?

Ⓐ sentence 2
Ⓑ sentence 4
Ⓒ sentence 7
Ⓓ sentence 9

Writing Strategies and Conventions

Name _____

Kayla wrote the letter below to her friend Rosie. The letter has some mistakes. Read the letter to answer Numbers 59 through 61.

Benchmark Assessment
Mid-Year

> Camp Pine Bluff
> Cedar Mountain, NC 28710
> July 10, _____
>
> Dear Rosie,
>
> [1] I hope you are having fun back home. [2] I am having a great time at summer camp. [3] It would be even better if you were here.
>
> [4] The horn blew at 6:00 A.M., when the sun was barely up. [5] That is how we start everyday around here. [6] We campers lined up and our counselors made sure we were all there. [7] We got into groups of 12, with each group picking a leader and getting supplies. [8] We covered ourselves with bug spray. [9] The food at camp is really good.
>
> [10] Then we set out on the trail. [11] The trail was narrow and windy. [12] At times the forest around us was thick. [13] Other times it wrapped around the edges of steep cliffs. [14] We had to be very careful and follow the many rules we had learned in order to be safe. [15] The hike was hard too. [16] It was almost five miles long and took about five hours in all.
>
> [17] The hike was filled with beautiful views. [18] Along the way we stopped to explore amazing waterfalls and caves. [19] We studied different trees. [20] We ran across many animals.
>
> [21] I hope someday you and I can go on a hike together. [22] I miss you!
>
> Your Best Friend,
> Kayla

Writing Strategies and Conventions

GO ON

Name _____

Benchmark Assessment
Mid-Year

59. Which transition word should be added to the beginning of sentence 3 to help connect the ideas in the paragraph?

   F However
   G Also
   H Furthermore
   I First

60. Which sentence is off topic and should be taken out of the second paragraph?

   A sentence 4
   B sentence 6
   C sentence 7
   D sentence 9

61. The writer wants to add the following sentence to the letter

   We saw twelve kinds of birds and took notes about each in our journals.

   Where should this detail be added to correctly organize the ideas?

   F after sentence 2
   G after sentence 5
   H after sentence 14
   I after sentence 20

Writing Strategies and Conventions

Name _____

Below is a first draft of a story that Javier wrote. The story has some mistakes. Read the story to answer Numbers 62 through 65.

Benchmark Assessment Mid-Year

The Tornado Warning

[1] When their parents said they were going out, Max and Josh were excited. [2] Amanda was coming over. [3] Amanda was an amazing babysitter. [4] Once she organized a neighborhood game of capture the flag. [5] No matter what, Amanda always brought fun.

[6] On this night, Amanda had paints. [7] Amanda was a high school student. [8] "Your parents said we can paint a picture on the wall in the basement," she told them.

[9] "You are kidding!" Max and Josh said.

[10] "No," said Amanda. [11] "They really did."

[12] The three got to work. [13] They painted the wall white. [14] Then they planned what to paint. [15] They decided on a pirate ship.

[16] They had just started to paint the pirates on the ship when they heard the sound of sirens.

[17] "What is that sound?" asked the boys, worried.

[18] "It is a tornado siren," said Amanda. [19] "That means a tornado has been seen in the area. [20] If we stay in the basement, we will be safe."

[21] So they forgot their worries and continued to paint.

[22] Max and Josh's parents came home soon after. [23] "We were worried," they said.

[24] "We were safe here in the basement," said Amanda. [25] "Unless, of course, you were worried about the pirates."

Writing Strategies and Conventions

Name _____

Benchmark Assessment — Mid-Year

62. Which sentence contains a detail that is unimportant to the story?

    Ⓐ sentence 1
    Ⓑ sentence 7
    Ⓒ sentence 8
    Ⓓ sentence 18

63. The writer wants to add this sentence to the first paragraph:

    Another time she brought water balloons for a water fight.

    Where should this sentence be added to keep the events of the story in order?

    Ⓕ after sentence 1
    Ⓖ after sentence 2
    Ⓗ after sentence 3
    Ⓘ after sentence 4

64. Which transition word should be added to the beginning of sentence 13 to help connect the ideas in the fifth paragraph?

    Ⓐ But
    Ⓑ However
    Ⓒ First
    Ⓓ Last

65. Which sentence should be added after sentence 20 to support the ideas in the eighth paragraph?

    Ⓕ But your basement is the best place to be in a tornado.
    Ⓖ The pirate scene had a boat, an island, and pirates.
    Ⓗ Both of the boys loved to draw and paint pictures.
    Ⓘ Their parents tried to call but there was no answer.

Writing Strategies and Conventions

GO ON

Name _____

Benchmark Assessment
Mid-Year

▶ Read the story "Where Was Everyone?" The story contains blanks. Choose the word or words that correctly complete Numbers 66 through 68.

Where Was Everyone?

Randy looked down the empty street. Since Tuesday, Randy had been in bed with the flu. He was finally feeling well. Today was the first day that his father would let him outside. Randy brought his kite to fly with his friends.

Randy searched for Rex, Mei-Lu, and Sara. __(66)__ were always at the park on Saturdays. Where was everyone? There didn't seem to be anyone at the park at all.

Randy ran home. He __(67)__ through the back door window and at the kitchen clock. It was 6:30 A.M. No wonder his __(68)__ could not be found. Randy had been so excited to play outside he didn't check the time before he left!

66. Which answer should go in blank (66)?
    Ⓐ Those
    Ⓑ Them
    Ⓒ They

67. Which answer should go in blank (67)?
    Ⓕ looks
    Ⓖ looked
    Ⓗ is looking

68. Which answer should go in blank (68)?
    Ⓐ friend's
    Ⓑ friendes
    Ⓒ friends

Writing Strategies and Conventions

GO ON

Name _____

Benchmark Assessment
Mid-Year

▶ Read the story "The Climb." The story contains blanks. Choose the word or words that correctly complete Numbers 69 through 71.

The Climb

Dave was determined. Today would be the day. He would climb the wall.

Usually when he went rock climbing at the (69)____, Dave got only halfway up the wall. Then suddenly he felt (70)____. He felt unable to climb any more. He had to stop.

Today, though, he thought of his older brother, Scott. Scott had told him, "Your mind says no before your body does. You can do it!"

Dave was halfway to the top. He took a deep breath of (71)____. He thought of his brother. He kept climbing, all the way to the top. He had done it!

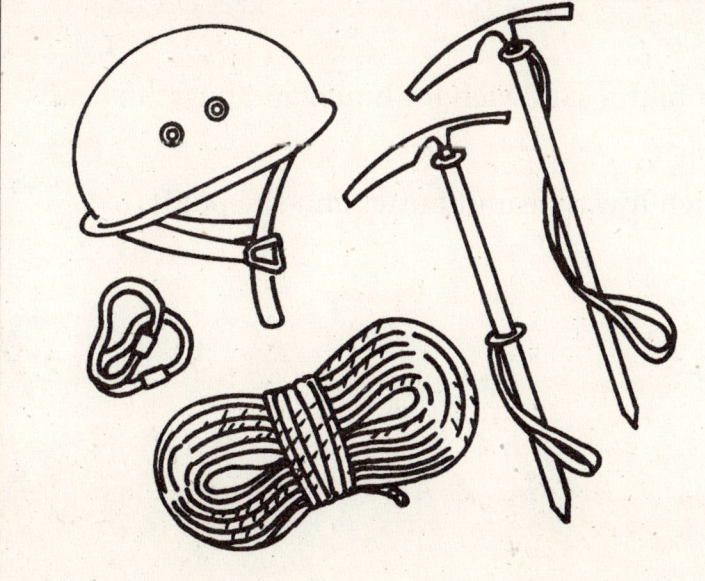

69. Which answer should go in blank (69)?
    Ⓕ red rock climbing club
    Ⓖ Red Rock Climbing Club
    Ⓗ Red rock climbing club

70. Which answer should go in blank (70)?
    Ⓐ powerless
    Ⓑ powerable
    Ⓒ powerment

71. Which answer should go in blank (71)?
    Ⓕ heir
    Ⓖ err
    Ⓗ air

Writing Strategies and Conventions

39

GO ON

Name _____

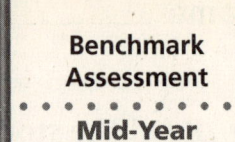

▶ **Read and answer Numbers 72 through 75.**

72. In which sentence below is all **capitalization** correct?

    Ⓐ Tina's cousin asked us, "can I come to new york with you?"

    Ⓑ Tina's cousin asked us, "can I come to New York with you?"

    Ⓒ Tina's cousin asked us, "Can I come to New York with you?"

73. In which sentence below is all **punctuation** correct?

    Ⓕ She packed pens, paper, and books into her school bag.

    Ⓖ She packed pens paper, and books into her school bag.

    Ⓗ She packed pens, paper, and books into her school bag

74. Combine the sentences below to make one sentence.

    > Annie made her lunch.
    > It was a peanut butter sandwich.
    > She put it in a paper bag.

    Which sentence correctly combines the sentences in the box?

    Ⓐ Annie made a sandwich and it was peanut butter and she put it in a paper bag.

    Ⓑ Annie made a peanut butter sandwich for lunch and put it in a paper bag.

    Ⓒ Annie made a sandwich it was peanut butter and she put it in a paper bag.

Writing Strategies and Conventions

Name _____

75. Put the ideas below together to create a sentence that makes sense.

> his model car
> before dinner
> when he found the kit
> Hong built

Which sentence below correctly combines the words from the box?

(F) Before dinner his model car when he found the kit Hong built.

(G) Hong built when he found the kit before dinner his model car.

(H) Hong built his model car when he found the kit before dinner.

Writing Strategies and Conventions

Name _____

Benchmark Assessment
Mid-Year

▶ For Numbers 76 through 80, read each sentence. If none of the underlined words are misspelled, choose the answer "No mistake."

76. Ⓐ We needed to retrace our steps.
    Ⓑ The house used solar power.
    Ⓒ His mother did not tolerate any siliness.
    Ⓓ No mistake

77. Ⓕ Look at the pretty raven in the sky!
    Ⓖ They gave coins to the poor orfin.
    Ⓗ I'd like to hear you defend your opinion.
    Ⓘ No mistake

78. Ⓐ The boy licked the cold icicle.
    Ⓑ Please hurry home for supper.
    Ⓒ Do you think the ostretch is a silly bird?
    Ⓓ No mistake

79. Ⓕ The bluebird hovvered over the bush.
    Ⓖ The farmer woke up at dawn.
    Ⓗ The fleet was destroyed at sea.
    Ⓘ No mistake

80. Ⓐ Dorothy loves to draw moonbeems.
    Ⓑ She has only one daughter.
    Ⓒ Can you pass the crayon?
    Ⓓ No mistake

Writing Strategies and Conventions

STOP

Name _____

Writing to a Prompt

Benchmark Assessment — Mid-Year

> Most of us have a favorite game or hobby that we enjoy.
> Think about a game or hobby that you enjoy.
> Now write to explain what you like about that game or hobby.

Planning Page

▶ Use this space to make your notes before you begin writing. The writing on this page will NOT be scored.

_____
_____
_____
_____
_____
_____
_____
_____
_____
_____
_____

Writing to a Prompt

GO ON

Name _____

Benchmark Assessment — Mid-Year

▶ **Begin writing here. The writing on this page and the next WILL be scored.**

Writing to a Prompt

GO ON

Name _____

Benchmark Assessment
Mid-Year

___

Writing to a Prompt

45

Oral Reading Fluency

Benchmark Assessment Mid-Year

Sam's mother was concerned because Sam would not eat his vegetables. He said that he didn't like how they tasted. Mom repeatedly told him that he had to eat his vegetables to grow up a strong and healthy individual. But Sam stubbornly refused.

Margaret, Sam's sister, attempted to help by encouraging Sam to eat vegetables, saying that they really taste delicious. Margaret's favorite vegetable is corn. She liked her corn with peppers and a pat of butter. But Sam wouldn't touch it. Margaret chewed on a fresh carrot, but Sam chose not to join her in chomping on one.

Mom and Margaret were stumped and could not decide what to do, but then Margaret had an idea. She winked at her mother. Mom smiled and nodded and they went into the kitchen, while Sam went outdoors to play.

Soon Sam came into the kitchen, sniffing the air. Something really smelled good! Freshly baked, piping hot cookies were sitting on the kitchen table. Sam ate three cookies and said they were the best he had ever tasted. They were very flavorful and very chewy. Mom and Margaret laughed, which surprised Sam, so he asked what the joke was.

Mom told him the cookies were made with lots of carrots, which made the cookies both chewy and sweet. Sam reconsidered his opinion about vegetables and began to try them at least one at every meal.

Some people think of bats as fearsome, but instead of being harmful, bats are quite interesting and helpful.

One surprising fact about bats is that they are the only mammals that truly fly. There are almost 1,000 different kinds of bats, and they all fly.

Bats have an unusual skill when it comes to finding their way around. Many kinds of bats don't see well. But they use their hearing in a very special way. They make a high-pitched sound and listen to its echo as it bounces off objects. Although a few kinds of bats do see and smell well, most kinds of bats use this unusual method of "seeing" as they fly and hunt.

Insects, not people, are the ones who should be scared of bats. One small brown bat can catch and eat up to 600 mosquitoes in a single hour. That's a skill you might be thankful for if you've ever had a mosquito bite. Bats also fertilize plants as they fly from one plant to the other, and they scatter plant seeds. Both of these actions help new plants to grow.

Each of us decides whether or not to be afraid of bats. The more you know about bats, the more you realize how helpful they are.

HARCOURT SCHOOL PUBLISHERS
STORYtown

Grade 4

Mid-Year Assessment

Benchmark Assessments

Harcourt
SCHOOL PUBLISHERS

www.harcourtschool.com

ISBN-13: 978-0-15-358768-9
ISBN-10: 0-15-358768-7

(Package of 12)

Grade 4 Benchmark Assessment
End-of-Year

Name _____ Date _____

Performance Summary

	Student Score
READING	
Reading Comprehension	
Multiple-Choice Items	_____/32
Short-Response Open-Ended Item	_____/2
Short-Response Open-Ended Item	_____/2
Extended-Response Open-Ended Item	_____/4
Vocabulary and Word Analysis	_____/20
Total Student Reading Score	_____/60
WRITING	
Writing Strategies and Conventions	_____/25
Writing Prompt	_____/6
ORAL READING FLUENCY	
Passage 1	_____ Words Correct Per Minute
Passage 2	_____ Words Correct Per Minute

(Bubble in the appropriate performance level.)

Reading

Below Basic	Basic (On-Level)	Proficient (On-Level)	Advanced
1–35	36–45	46–55	56–60
○	○	○	○

Writing Conventions

Below Basic	Basic (On-Level)	Proficient (On-Level)	Advanced
1–10	11–15	16–19	20–25
○	○	○	○

Writing Prompt

Below Basic	Basic (On-Level)	Proficient (On-Level)	Advanced
1–2	3–4	5	6
○	○	○	○

Oral Reading Fluency

25th Percentile	50th Percentile	75th Percentile	90th Percentile
98 WCPM	123 WCPM	152 WCPM	180 WCPM
○	○	○	○

For permission to reprint copyrighted material, grateful acknowledgment is made to the following sources:

Highlights for Children, Inc., Columbus, Ohio: From "Fly High, Bessie Coleman" by Jane Sutcliffe in *Highlights for Children* Magazine, February 2004. Text copyright © 2004 by Highlights for Children, Inc.

Little, Brown & Company, Inc.: From *Once Inside the Library* (Retitled: "The Library") by Barbara Huff. Text copyright © 1957 by Barbara A. Huff; text copyright © renewed 1985 by Barbara A. Huff.

Copyright © by Harcourt, Inc.

All rights reserved. No part of this publication may be reproduced or transmitted in any form or by any means, electronic or mechanical, including photocopy, recording, or any information storage and retrieval system, without permission in writing from the publisher.

Permission is hereby granted to individuals using the corresponding student's textbook or kit as the major vehicle for regular classroom instruction to photocopy entire pages from this publication in classroom quantities for instructional use and not for resale. Requests for information on other matters regarding duplication of this work should be addressed to School Permissions and Copyrights, Harcourt, Inc., 6277 Sea Harbor Drive, Orlando, Florida 32887-6777. Fax: 407-345-2418.

HARCOURT and the Harcourt Logo are trademarks of Harcourt, Inc., registered in the United States of America and/or other jurisdictions.

Printed in the United States of America

ISBN 10 0-15-358768-7   ISBN 13 978-0-15-358768-9

1 2 3 4 5 6 7 8 9 10   073   16 15 14 13 12 11 10 09 08 07

If you have received these materials as examination copies free of charge, Harcourt School Publishers retains title to the materials and they may not be resold. Resale of examination copies is strictly prohibited and is illegal.

Possession of this publication in print format does not entitle users to convert this publication, or any portion of it, into electronic format.

Name _____

Reading Comprehension

▶ Read the story "Lost Pet" before answering Numbers 1 through 7.

Lost Pet

"Ziggy!" Jasmine stood on the porch and called her cat, but no orange-and-white tabby strolled out from behind the shrubs, or from under the minivan in the driveway.

Jasmine checked under her bed and under her computer table.

"Ziggy, where are you hiding?"

Searching inside the house had proved fruitless, so Jasmine returned to the yard, calling and calling her cat as she combed every hiding place she could remember. Ziggy had never been missing for so long before. Worried, Jasmine decided to ask her parents for help.

She found her mother in the den. "Mom, have you seen Ziggy?" she asked.

"Not since early this morning," her mother replied.

Next, Jasmine asked her father the same question.

"I saw Ziggy strolling through the flowerbed, but that was hours ago," he said.

By now, Jasmine was sure Ziggy had gotten lost. It was time to take action, so she took a sheet of paper, sketched a picture of Ziggy, and then wrote "Lost Cat" and her phone number below the drawing. She included a detailed description of her cat: large orange tabby, golden eyes, and fluffy coat of fur. Jasmine photocopied the posters and asked her mother to help her hang them up around the neighborhood. Then they went home to wait for a call.

Within two hours, she received a phone call in answer to her ad. A friendly voice on the other line said, "My name is Mrs. Garcia, and I believe I have Ziggy."

Jasmine was so excited that she jumped up and down. Then she remembered to ask Mrs. Garcia for her address and phone number. Finally, she asked what had happened.

"A huge orange tabby just strolled into my yard this afternoon. He has been resting on the porch, and he looks very comfortable," she added.

"I'll be right over to see if it's Ziggy," Jasmine exclaimed. She and her parents climbed into their minivan and drove to Mrs. Garcia's house.

Once Jasmine and her parents got to Mrs. Garcia's house, they discovered that the tabby was indeed Jasmine's lost Ziggy. Jasmine immediately scooped him up in her arms, nuzzled him, and buried her face in the soft fur of his neck. Ziggy closed his eyes and purred, as if his wandering away and being found again had been the most natural thing in the world.

Jasmine slipped the cat into his carrier, snapped the latch shut, and slid the carrier into the minivan. Her parents thanked Mrs. Garcia for her help, and drove their daughter and her beloved pet back home.

The next afternoon, Jasmine spotted Mrs. Garcia walking down the street. Mrs. Garcia wore a worried expression on her face.

Jasmine waved to her and walked over. "Is something wrong?" she asked.

"Yes, Jasmine. It's odd, coming so soon after your adventure with Ziggy, but today my dog, Diego, is missing.

"Tell me about him," Jasmine asked. Mrs. Garcia described Diego's looks and personality.

"Is he a beagle?" Jasmine asked, and Mrs. Garcia nodded yes.

"I can help," Jasmine said. "I'll make posters for you and put them up."

Jasmine went home and hurriedly sketched a picture of a beagle. She added Mrs. Garcia's phone number, Diego's name and description, and some details about how he got lost. Again she made photocopies, and again her mother helped her hang them up.

That evening, Mrs. Garcia called Jasmine with the happy report that someone had identified a lost beagle in his neighborhood as Diego.

"You used your experience with Ziggy to help me," said Mrs. Garcia. "I really appreciate it. I'd like to invite you and your parents over tomorrow to meet Diego and to have some cookies," she continued.

"I look forward to it," Jasmine replied. "I'm so happy that both of our stories had happy endings!"

Name _____

Benchmark Assessment
End-of-Year

▶ Now answer Numbers 1 through 7. Base your answers on the story "Lost Pet."

1. How are Jasmine and Mrs. Garcia ALIKE?
   - Ⓐ Both have very large pets.
   - Ⓑ Both know how to draw animals.
   - Ⓒ Both lose their pets for a short time.
   - Ⓓ Both have a cat and a dog in their homes.

2. Why does Jasmine draw a picture of Ziggy?
   - Ⓕ to show how much she loves her cat
   - Ⓖ to help people recognize Ziggy if they find him
   - Ⓗ to encourage the neighbors to have cats as pets
   - Ⓘ to give to her neighbor Mrs. Garcia

3. What happens BEFORE Jasmine offers to help Mrs. Garcia?
   - Ⓐ Jasmine asks if Mrs. Garcia's dog is a beagle.
   - Ⓑ Jasmine sketches pictures of a beagle.
   - Ⓒ Mrs. Garcia reports that someone found a lost beagle.
   - Ⓓ Mrs. Garcia invites Jasmine to have some cookies.

4. Where does Mrs. Garcia find Ziggy?
   - Ⓕ on her porch
   - Ⓖ in her garden
   - Ⓗ on the sidewalk
   - Ⓘ in her neighborhood

Reading Comprehension

GO ON

Name _____

5. Read this sentence from the story.

   Her parents thanked Mrs. Garcia for her help, and drove their daughter and her beloved pet back home.

   Which word means about the SAME as *beloved* in this sentence?

   Ⓐ tired
   Ⓑ playful
   Ⓒ treasured
   Ⓓ mischievous

6. What will Mrs. Garcia MOST LIKELY do if Diego gets lost again?

   Ⓕ wait for him to come home
   Ⓖ call Jasmine to help her
   Ⓗ check in her flowerbed
   Ⓘ call the local pet shelter

Reading Comprehension

Name _____

Benchmark Assessment
End-of-Year

7. What is Jasmine's main problem in this story, and how is it solved? Base your answer on details from the story.

_____
_____
_____
_____
_____
_____
_____
_____

Reading Comprehension

Name _____

Read the article "Recycling" before answering Numbers 8 through 15.

Recycling

Have you ever used an old bag or box? If so, you have recycled. One way to recycle is to reuse old things in new ways. For example, you can make a desk organizer out of an egg carton, use the Sunday comics to wrap a present, or jot notes on the back of an old envelope.

Many cities recycle. Residents put the trash that can be recycled into special bins. Glass, plastic, newspaper, some metals, and sometimes foam are among the materials that are recycled. The bins are put out with the trash, and picked up by sanitation workers. They are then sorted and taken to processing plants and factories to make new products. Therefore, recycling means less garbage.

What becomes of our recycled objects? Many new products are made from old ones. For example, old foam is shredded and pressed together into a jumble of many-colored foam, which is stuffed into pillows or used as carpet padding. Old paper turns up on store shelves as paper towels, cardboard, pet beds, and even as copier paper. Glass bottles and jars may be crushed into tiny pieces and used to pave roads, or they may be ground up into sand-size particles that are used on golf courses.

Recycled plastic has many uses. It is used to make toys, pens, pencils, fences, flowerpots, and outdoor furniture. Some kinds of plastic are even used to make soft, warm clothes!

It is important to recycle. It helps us to have less garbage. It also keeps us from wasting the Earth's trees and metals. When we recycle, we are being smart and taking care of the Earth, ourselves, and our future.

Look at the graph to see how many tons of paper each city recycles in a year.

Name _____

Benchmark Assessment
End-of-Year

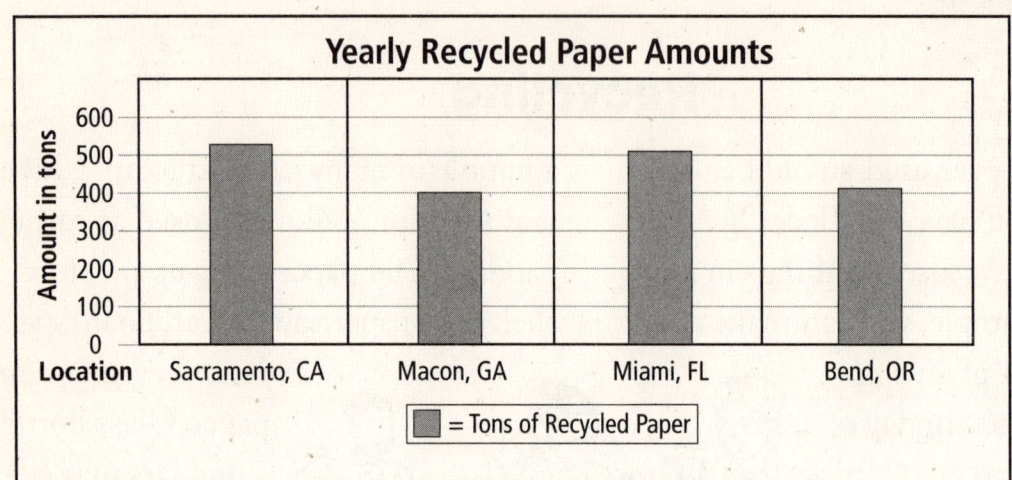

Reading Comprehension

Name _____

Benchmark Assessment
End-of-Year

▶ Now answer Numbers 8 through 15. Base your answers on the article "Recycling."

8. Which reason BEST tells why the author wrote this article?
   Ⓐ to inform readers about the benefits of recycling
   Ⓑ to let readers know how to find a recycling center
   Ⓒ to tell an entertaining story about recycling in one city
   Ⓓ to convince readers to buy products made from garbage

9. According to the article, what can people do at home to help reduce garbage?
   Ⓕ throw out materials
   Ⓖ grind up glass
   Ⓗ reuse materials
   Ⓘ crush up jars

10. According to the article, what will be the MAIN problem if people choose not to recycle?
    Ⓐ The earth's trees and metals will be wasted.
    Ⓑ No new products will be developed.
    Ⓒ Cities will have to hire more sanitation workers.
    Ⓓ Cities will have to distribute more recycle bins.

Reading Comprehension

GO ON

Name _____

Benchmark Assessment
End-of-Year

11. Read this sentence from the article.

    > For example, old foam is shredded and pressed together into a jumble of many-colored foam, which is stuffed into pillows or used as carpet padding.

    What does the word *jumble* mean in this sentence?

    F pattern
    G mixture
    H picture
    I order

12. Which of the following sentences from the article is an OPINION and not a fact?

    A "One way to recycle is to use old things in new ways."
    B "Residents put the trash that can be recycled into special bins."
    C "Some kinds of plastic are even used to make soft, warm clothes!"
    D "It is important to recycle."

13. According to the graph, which city recycled the most paper?

    F Bend, OR
    G Macon, GA
    H Miami, FL
    I Sacramento, CA

14. According to the graph, which city recycled 400 tons of paper?

    A Bend, OR
    B Macon, GA
    C Miami, FL
    D Sacramento, CA

Reading Comprehension

GO ON

Name _____

Benchmark Assessment
End-of-Year

15. According to the article, what are TWO benefits of recycling? Use details and information from the article to support your answer.

READ
THINK
EXPLAIN

_____
_____
_____
_____
_____
_____
_____

Reading Comprehension

GO ON

Name _____

Benchmark Assessment
End-of-Year

▶ Read the poem "The Library" before answering Numbers 16 through 19.

The Library
By Barbara A. Huff

It looks like any building
When you pass it on the street,
Made of stone and glass and marble,
Made of iron and concrete.

But once inside you can ride
A camel or a train,
Visit Rome, Siam, or Nome,
Feel a hurricane,
Meet a king, learn to sing,
How to bake a pie,
Go to sea, plant a tree,
Find how airplanes fly,
Train a horse, and of course
Have all the dogs you'd like,
See the moon, a sandy dune,
Or catch a whopping pike.
Everything that books can bring
You'll find inside those walls.
A world is there for you to share
When adventure calls.

You cannot tell its magic
By the way the building looks,
But there's wonderment within it,
The wonderment of books.

Reading Comprehension

© Harcourt • Grade 4

Name _____

**Benchmark Assessment
End-of-Year**

▶ Now answer Numbers 16 through 19. Base your answers on the poem "The Library."

16. Read these lines from the poem.

    **But once inside you can ride
    A camel or a train,**

    What is the author referring to in these lines?

    Ⓕ books about camels or trains
    Ⓖ buying a train ticket
    Ⓗ petting a camel
    Ⓘ libraries near train tracks

17. To what does the author compare the library?

    Ⓐ other buildings
    Ⓑ people
    Ⓒ cities
    Ⓓ storms

18. Read these lines from the poem.

    **See the moon, a sandy dune,
    Or catch a whopping pike.**

    What does *whopping* mean in this line?

    Ⓕ travels
    Ⓖ very busy
    Ⓗ in the desert
    Ⓘ very large

Reading Comprehension

19. Based on the poem, what can you tell about the author?

    Ⓐ She likes to read.
    Ⓑ She likes to eat.
    Ⓒ She likes to write.
    Ⓓ She likes to cook.

Name _____

Benchmark Assessment
End-of-Year

▶ Read the article "Making a Journal" before answering Numbers 20 through 24.

Making a Journal

Mrs. Clark's students are making journals about their state. Each student will write five amazing facts about where they live and draw pictures about their state. Read Mrs. Clark's directions for making the journal.

Supplies:
- 10 pieces of unlined white paper
- 2 pieces of colored paper
- Crayons and markers

Directions:

On a piece of colored paper, complete the following tasks
- Write the title of your journal at the top of the page.
- Write your name at the bottom of the page.
- Draw a picture of your state.
- Place this page on top of the 10 pieces of white paper.
- Place the other piece of colored paper beneath the white papers.

After each student organizes his or her journal, Mrs. Clark punches holes in the journal pages so that each student can put the pages in order into a small binder. Then Mrs. Clark writes on the chalkboard what students should put in the journal.

Journal Information:
- On one journal page, write an amazing fact about your state.
- On the page next to it, draw a picture to illustrate that fact.
- You should have 5 amazing facts.

Parents' Night

When all students have completed their journals, Mrs. Clark will put the journals on display on special tables for visitors to see on Parents' Night.

Name _____

▶ Now answer Numbers 20 through 24. Base your answers on the article "Making a Journal."

Benchmark Assessment
End-of-Year

20. Read this phrase from the article.

   "10 pieces of unlined white paper"

   What does the prefix *un–* suggest that the word *unlined* means in this sentence?

   Ⓕ below the lines
   Ⓖ having many lines
   Ⓗ between the lines
   Ⓘ not having lines

21. Which section tells the reader what is needed to make the journal?

   Ⓐ Supplies
   Ⓑ Directions
   Ⓒ Journal Information
   Ⓓ Parents' Night

22. Why does Mrs. Clark MOST LIKELY write "Journal Information" on the chalkboard?

   Ⓕ so she will remember what goes in the journals
   Ⓖ so students know what to put in their journals
   Ⓗ so students know what to bring for Parents' Night
   Ⓘ so she will know how to grade the journals

Reading Comprehension

GO ON

Name _____

23. Read this sentence from the article.

   On the journal page next to it, draw a picture to illustrate that fact.

   What does *illustrate* mean in this sentence?
   Ⓐ to locate
   Ⓑ to show
   Ⓒ to name
   Ⓓ to prove

24. Which BEST describes how the article is organized?
   Ⓕ It describes the events of Parents' Night.
   Ⓖ It proves the importance of using journal.
   Ⓗ It compares drawing with making a journal.
   Ⓘ It tells the steps in order to make a journal.

Read the story "Gathering Food" before answering Numbers 25 through 29.

Gathering Food

From the moment Adahy caught a glimpse of the big orange sun appearing over the mountain tops, he was positive that today would be a great day. Adahy and his friends would gather acorns to store for the winter months, an important task because the acorns would nourish the people in the cave when food was scarce.

Adahy anticipated his friends emerging from the cave, and then the three of them would start searching for acorns. As Adahy stared at the giant oak and hickory trees that surrounded the cave, he contemplated the various tasks assigned to each person who lived in the cave. The men constructed tools for hunting and fishing, while the women crafted pots and gathered berries, roots, and seeds to eat during winter.

Finally, Tooantuh and Sheasequat appeared. Sheasequat glanced at Adahy's empty hands and asked, "Adahy, do you have a pot to put the acorns in?"

"Oh, I forgot, but I will get it now," said Adahy. He disappeared into the cave and quickly returned with two large clay pots.

Adahy, Tooantuh, and Sheasequat started out on the path into the forest. The lofty trees towered over the boys, forming a tunnel into the woods. The boys were cautious about staying together and on the path. They listened closely to the sounds of the forest, straining their ears to hear squirrels chattering, a telltale sign of nearby acorns.

"Stop!" Tooantuh whispered, holding out his hand. "I think I hear them." The boys halted, looked up, and spotted several squirrels scampering among the trees.

"There they are," Sheasequat said. "Now we are sure to find what we need."

As squirrels scurried over their heads, Sheasequat, Tooantuh, and Adahy searched for acorns. They explored the

forest around them and uncovered acorns under dried leaves and twigs. The squirrels found the acorns, too, in the oak branches above. Together the boys and the squirrels collected food for the winter; the squirrels would hoard them in their nests, while the people of the cave would store them in dirt holes to cool and preserve them.

When their pots were bursting with acorns, the boys returned to the path that would take them back to the cave. They would present the overflowing pots to Adsila, the food keeper, when they arrived.

"Adsila," they called proudly as they entered the cave. "Look what we have found."

Adsila turned to the boys and smiled. "You have done a great job. These acorns will feed many of us when it begins to snow. See what the women have collected for us." She gestured toward the holes in the cave floor.

Adahy and his friends peered into one of the holes in the dirt and saw seeds, roots, and nuts. The boys' pots of acorns made a significant contribution to the stores of winter food and would require a new hole. This winter, no one in the cave would go hungry.

Adahy was full of pride because he and his friends were helping to feed the cave families. He strolled out the cave entrance and gazed at the yellow sun setting behind the mountain tops against the rosy sky. Tomorrow would be an excellent day to forage for more food with Sheasequat and Tooantuh.

Name _____

Benchmark Assessment
End-of-Year

▶ Now answer Numbers 25 through 29. Base your answers on the story "Gathering Food."

25. Where does this story MOSTLY take place?
    Ⓐ near a stream
    Ⓑ on a trail
    Ⓒ in a cave
    Ⓓ in a tree

26. What problem does Adahy face as he prepares for his task?
    Ⓕ He forgets his fishing tool.
    Ⓖ He forgets his clay pots.
    Ⓗ His friends disappear.
    Ⓘ His friends do not help him.

27. Read this sentence from the story.

    They listened closely to the sounds of the forest, straining their ears to hear squirrels chattering, a telltale sign of nearby acorns.

    What is the BEST way to paraphrase this sentence?
    Ⓐ The squirrel's noises would lead them to acorns.
    Ⓑ The squirrel's noises would cause acorns to drop from the trees.
    Ⓒ The squirrels would have already collected the acorns.
    Ⓓ The squirrels would be so noisy that they would have to take another path.

Reading Comprehension

21

GO ON

© Harcourt • Grade 4

28. Which word BEST describes Adahy and the other members of the cave families?

   F forgetful
   G lazy
   H over-confident
   I hard-working

29. Which BEST describes the theme of the story?

   A Caring for the environment makes the world a better place.
   B Enjoying the simple things in life is important.
   C Walking in nature results in happiness.
   D Working together pays off in the end.

Fly High, Bessie Coleman

by Jane Sutcliffe

Two thousand people sat with their faces turned to the sky. High above the airfield, a pilot had just finished carving a crisp figure eight in the air. Suddenly, the plane seemed to stumble. Twisting and turning, it began to fall from the sky. The crowd watched in horror. Had something happened to the pilot?

But the woman in the cockpit of the plane on October 15, 1922, was in perfect control. Only two hundred feet above the ground she straightened out the tumbling aircraft and soared back into the sky. By the time she landed her plane, the crowd was on its feet, roaring with delight. Everyone cheered for Bessie Coleman, the first licensed black pilot in the world.

Coleman, in uniform, stands on the runner of a Model T Ford. The nose and right wing of her plane are to her left.

Growing Up

Bessie Coleman was born on January 26, 1892. She was a bright girl and a star pupil in school. In Waxahachie, Texas, where Bessie grew up, black children and white children attended different schools. Each year Bessie's school closed for months at a time. Instead of studying, the children joined their parents picking cotton on big plantations. Bessie's mother was proud of her daughter's sharp mind. She didn't want Bessie to spend her life picking cotton, and urged her to do something special with her life.

Learning to Fly

In 1915, when she was 23, Bessie Coleman moved to Chicago. She found a job as a manicurist in a men's barbershop. Coleman loved her job and the interesting people she met there. After the United States entered World War I in 1917, soldiers returning from the war often came to the shop. Coleman was fascinated by their stories of daredevil pilots. She read everything she could about airplanes and flying. She later recalled, "All the articles I read finally convinced me I should be up there flying and not just reading about it."

Bessie Coleman asked some of Chicago's pilots for lessons. They refused. No one thought that an African American woman could learn to fly.

In desperation, Coleman asked Robert Abbott for help. Abbott owned Chicago's African American newspaper, *The Chicago Defender*. He had often promised to help members of the black community with their problems. Abbott told Coleman to forget about learning to fly in the United States. Go to France, he said to her, where no one would care if her skin was black or white.

So she did. First Coleman learned to speak French. Then she applied to a French flying school and was accepted. On November 20, 1920, Coleman sailed for France, where she spent the next seven months taking flying lessons. She learned to fly straight and level, and to turn and bank the plane. She practiced making perfect landings. On a second trip to Europe, she spent months mastering rolls, loops, and spins. These were the tricks she would need if she planned to make her living as a performing pilot.

Performing in Airshows

Coleman returned to the United States in the summer of 1922. Wherever she performed, other African Americans wanted to know where they, too, could learn to fly. It was a question that made Coleman sad. She hoped that she could make enough money from her airshows to buy her own plane. Then she could open a school so everyone would have a chance to feel the freedom she felt in the sky.

By early 1923, Coleman was close to her goal. She had saved her money and bought a plane. Then, as she was flying to an airshow in California, her engine stalled. The brand-new plane crashed to the ground.

Coleman suffered a broken leg and three broken ribs. Still, she refused to quit. "Tell them all that as soon as I can walk I'm going to fly!" she wrote to friends and fans.

Coleman's pilot license was issued on June 15, 1921, in France. The year of her birth is incorrect. Bessie Coleman was born in 1892, not 1896.

Many people, both black and white, were very impressed by Coleman's determination. A white businessman helped her buy another plane. By 1926, Coleman was back where she had been before the crash. She wrote to her sister, "I am right on the threshold of opening a school."

In 1929, three years after her death, the Bessie Coleman Aero Clubs were formed. The clubs encouraged and trained African American pilots—just as Coleman had hoped to do. In 1931, the clubs sponsored the first All-African-American airshow. Bessie Coleman would have been proud.

Name _____

Now answer Numbers 30 through 35. Base your answers on the article "Fly High, Bessie Coleman."

30. Which section of the article BEST explains how Bessie finds flying lessons?

    Ⓕ Growing Up

    Ⓖ Learning to Fly

    Ⓗ Performing in Air Shows

    Ⓘ the introduction

31. Which sentence from the article is an OPINION and not a fact?

    Ⓐ "Bessie Coleman would have been proud."

    Ⓑ "She had saved her money and bought a plane."

    Ⓒ "Then, as she was flying to an airshow in California, her engine stalled."

    Ⓓ "Coleman suffered a broken leg and three broken ribs."

32. Which reason BEST tells why the author wrote this article?

    Ⓕ to persuade others to attend airshows

    Ⓖ to prove that France has the best pilot schools

    Ⓗ to describe a person who followed her dream and made it come true

    Ⓘ to explain that if you are different, it is difficult to get what you want

Reading Comprehension

33. Which BEST describes how the article is organized?

   A It tells the steps one must go through in order to become a famous pilot.

   B It explains problems in learning to fly and how the problems are solved.

   C It compares and contrasts flying with other daring performances.

   D It explains the important events of one person's life in order.

34. What would Bessie MOST LIKELY have done if she had lived longer?

   F She would have gone back to France to learn more about flying.

   G She would have taught other African Americans how to fly.

   H She would have stopped writing letters to her sister.

   I She would have gone back to being a manicurist.

Name _____

Benchmark Assessment
End-of-Year

35. Write about the character traits that made Bessie Coleman a good pilot, and explain why those traits are important. Use information from the article to support your answer.

_____
_____
_____
_____
_____
_____
_____
_____
_____
_____
_____
_____
_____
_____

Name _____

Vocabulary and Word Analysis

Benchmark Assessment
End-of-Year

▶ For Numbers 36 through 49, choose the word that best completes each sentence.

36. All guests appreciate a _____ meal.
    - Ⓐ hearty
    - Ⓑ cordially
    - Ⓒ resolved
    - Ⓓ pathetic

37. The inventor liked to _____ in his lab.
    - Ⓕ tinker
    - Ⓖ insisted
    - Ⓗ declared
    - Ⓘ journey

38. Some monkeys can be very _____.
    - Ⓐ bountiful
    - Ⓑ mischievous
    - Ⓒ ancestors
    - Ⓓ hoaxer

39. He was slowly _____ from his nap.
    - Ⓕ gloated
    - Ⓖ forged
    - Ⓗ roused
    - Ⓘ trampled

Vocabulary and Word Analysis

GO ON

Name _____

Benchmark Assessment
End-of-Year

40. The students _____ waited for the test results.
    - (A) participate
    - (B) distressed
    - (C) inadvertently
    - (D) anxiously

41. The jam _____ of several kinds of berries.
    - (F) comforted
    - (G) burst
    - (H) snatched
    - (I) consisted

42. Carmen never _____ her friends' good qualities.
    - (A) recognizes
    - (B) prideful
    - (C) extracts
    - (D) remarkable

43. The last point gave the home team a great _____.
    - (F) advantage
    - (G) huddle
    - (H) withstand
    - (I) suspicion

44. The crowd admired the rich and _____ carriage.
    - (A) eerie
    - (B) submerged
    - (C) elegant
    - (D) sentries

Vocabulary and Word Analysis

GO ON

Name _____

Benchmark Assessment
End-of-Year

45. Most successful people are _____ to their goals.
    - Ⓕ massive
    - Ⓖ dedicated
    - Ⓗ memorable
    - Ⓘ dainty

46. How many _____ do you think go into a jar of jam?
    - Ⓐ berry
    - Ⓑ berrys
    - Ⓒ berries
    - Ⓓ berriest

47. You have to go underground to take the _____.
    - Ⓕ roadway
    - Ⓖ subway
    - Ⓗ highway
    - Ⓘ byway

48. The lawyer did his best to prove that the _____ was innocent.
    - Ⓐ defend
    - Ⓑ defensive
    - Ⓒ defendant
    - Ⓓ defer

49. The boy had _____ hard for the exam.
    - Ⓕ study
    - Ⓖ studies
    - Ⓗ studied
    - Ⓘ studious

Vocabulary and Word Analysis

GO ON

Name _____

Benchmark Assessment
End-of-Year

▶ **Read and answer Numbers 50 through 55.**

50. Which word means the SAME as *brave*?
    - Ⓐ cowardly
    - Ⓑ fearless
    - Ⓒ abrupt
    - Ⓓ tragic

51. Which word means the SAME as *loyal*?
    - Ⓕ mature
    - Ⓖ friendly
    - Ⓗ kindly
    - Ⓘ faithful

52. Which word means the SAME as *annoy*?
    - Ⓐ listen
    - Ⓑ bother
    - Ⓒ absorb
    - Ⓓ remain

53. Which word means the OPPOSITE of *work*?
    - Ⓕ grasp
    - Ⓖ rest
    - Ⓗ free
    - Ⓘ trail

54. Which word means the OPPOSITE of *argue*?
    - Ⓐ agree
    - Ⓑ pretend
    - Ⓒ meddle
    - Ⓓ collapse

Vocabulary and Word Analysis

GO ON

© Harcourt • Grade 4

Name _____

55. Which word means the OPPOSITE of *bright*?
    Ⓕ lazy
    Ⓖ dim
    Ⓗ broke
    Ⓘ flimsy

Vocabulary and Word Analysis

Name _____

Writing Strategies and Conventions

▶ Below is a first draft of a story that Sasha wrote about living on a farm. The story has some mistakes. Read the story to answer Numbers 56 through 58.

→ ⟦1⟧ My family lives on a farm. ⟦2⟧ The farm is big, so everyone has a lot of chores to do. ⟦3⟧ My sister and I wake up before the sun rises. ⟦4⟧ First, we feed the dog Max and the cat Henry. ⟦5⟧ Then we put on boots and go to the barn. ⟦6⟧ We use a flashlight to find the way.

→ ⟦7⟧ All of the animals are hungry in the morning. ⟦8⟧ We feed the chickens first. ⟦9⟧ One of our cows just had a baby calf. ⟦10⟧ We named the calf Brownie. ⟦11⟧ She needs a lot of extra attention.

→ ⟦12⟧ It is important to make sure all the animals have plenty of water. ⟦13⟧ We also make sure their stalls are clean. ⟦14⟧ Our last chore is gathering the eggs from the chicken coop for breakfast.

→ ⟦15⟧ After we're done with chores, we eat breakfast with Mom and Dad. ⟦16⟧ Then we pack our lunches and go to school. ⟦17⟧ The school bus picks us up on the country road.

→ ⟦18⟧ Mom and Dad do the rest of the chores while we are at school. ⟦19⟧ They take care of the fields where we grow corn and beans. ⟦20⟧ When we get home from school, we do our homework. ⟦21⟧ Our neighbor grows wheat on his farm. ⟦22⟧ When we're done with our homework, I help Mom make dinner, and we all eat together.

Benchmark Assessment
End-of-Year

Writing Strategies and Conventions

GO ON

Name _____

Benchmark Assessment
End-of-Year

56. Which sentence contains a detail that is unimportant to the story?

    Ⓐ sentence 13
    Ⓑ sentence 9
    Ⓒ sentence 21
    Ⓓ sentence 2

57. The writer wants to add the following sentence to the second paragraph of the story:

    Then we milk the cows so we have fresh milk for breakfast.

    Where should this sentence be added to keep the events of the story in order?

    Ⓕ after sentence 3
    Ⓖ after sentence 16
    Ⓗ after sentence 21
    Ⓘ after sentence 8

58. Which sentence below should be added after sentence 13 to support the ideas in the third paragraph?

    Ⓐ Cleaning the stalls is my least favorite chore.
    Ⓑ My sister likes working in the barn.
    Ⓒ Sometimes my father lets the pigs roam around the farm.
    Ⓓ I like to write stories about the animals.

Writing Strategies and Conventions

GO ON

Name _____

Benchmark Assessment
End-of-Year

▶ Alana wrote the letter below to her friend Evan. The letter has some mistakes. Read the letter to answer Numbers 59 through 61.

3867 Strain Ridge Avenue
Dallas, TX 72700
April 4, 20____

Dear Evan,

→ ⬜1 Thank you for the birthday card. ⬜2 Guess what my parents gave me for my birthday? ⬜3 They took me for a ride in a hot-air balloon!

→ ⬜4 On my birthday, we went to the park where the balloons take off and met our pilot. ⬜5 Her name was Susan. ⬜6 My aunt's name is Susan too. ⬜7 She showed us how to get into the basket that the pilot and passengers ride in. ⬜8 I thought the basket would be too small for everyone to fit in. ⬜9 It was just the right size.

→ ⬜10 Susan filled the balloon with hot air, and we took off! ⬜11 The balloon lifted us off the ground. ⬜12 Soon we were very high in the air. ⬜13 We drifted over the park and over my house. ⬜14 Susan turned off the burners and we floated over the city. ⬜15 It was very peaceful.

→ ⬜16 Soon it was time to land, though, so Susan let some of the hot air out of the balloon and we sank to the ground. ⬜17 We landed in the park and went home.

→ ⬜18 I took a lot of pictures. ⬜19 Would you like to come over to my house to see them? ⬜20 I hope that you can go on a balloon ride someday too!

Your Best Friend,
Alana

Writing Strategies and Conventions

GO ON

59. Which sentence is off-topic and should be taken out of the second paragraph?

- Ⓕ sentence 4
- Ⓖ sentence 6
- Ⓗ sentence 8
- Ⓘ sentence 9

60. Which sentence below should be added before sentence 16 to support the idea in the fourth paragraph?

- Ⓐ The pilot wasn't nervous at all.
- Ⓑ I didn't want the ride to end.
- Ⓒ The weather was cloudy and cool.
- Ⓓ I held my mother's hand the whole time.

61. Which transition word should be added to the beginning of sentence 9 to help connect the ideas in the paragraph?

- Ⓕ Therefore
- Ⓖ Moreover
- Ⓗ However
- Ⓘ Next

Name _____

Read Michael's story about visiting his grandparents' house. The story has some mistakes. Read the story to answer Numbers 62 through 65.

Benchmark Assessment
End-of-Year

→ [1] During winter break, I visit my grandparents. [2] Sometimes I help Grandpa fix things around the house. [3] Sometimes we go ice-skating. [4] However, my favorite thing to do is bake cookies with Grandma.

→ [5] My grandma's kitchen is big with lots of windows. [6] We start by getting all our ingredients together. [7] We mix flour, salt, and baking powder in one bowl. [8] We mix butter, sugar, and eggs in another bowl. [9] Finally, we mix everything together and stir in the chocolate chips. [10] I roll the dough into balls and set them on a cookie sheet. [11] Grandma puts the sheet in the oven and we wait for the cookies to bake.

→ [12] The hardest part is waiting for the cookies to come out of the oven. [13] They smell so delicious! [14] We put the cookies on a rack to cool.

→ [15] Grandma always lets me have one warm cookie while we're baking. [16] Grandpa usually comes in and steals three cookies. [17] Grandma tells him he has to save some for later. [18] Grandpa just laughs and pours himself a glass of milk.

→ [19] I like visiting my grandparents. [20] I always have lots of fun!

Name _____

Benchmark Assessment
End-of-Year

62. Which sentence below should be added before sentence 14 to support the idea in the third paragraph?

    Ⓐ When the timer rings, we know the cookies are done.
    Ⓑ Grandma and I talk about school while we're baking.
    Ⓒ Grandma's oven is white, so we try to keep it clean.
    Ⓓ It has to be very cold outside to go ice-skating.

63. The writer wants to add the following sentence to the story:

    Sometimes we make peanut butter or oatmeal cookies, but my favorite kind is chocolate chip.

    Where should this detail be added to correctly organize the ideas?

    Ⓕ after sentence 2
    Ⓖ after sentence 4
    Ⓗ after sentence 12
    Ⓘ after sentence 17

64. Which sentence is off-topic and should be taken out of the second paragraph?

    Ⓐ sentence 2
    Ⓑ sentence 5
    Ⓒ sentence 11
    Ⓓ sentence 15

65. Which event below could be added after the fourth paragraph to keep the story focused on the main idea?

    Ⓕ Sharing the cookies with neighbors
    Ⓖ Helping Grandpa put up a birdhouse
    Ⓗ Measuring the flour for the cookies
    Ⓘ A trip to the skating rink

Writing Strategies and Conventions

GO ON

Name _____

Benchmark Assessment • End-of-Year

▶ Read the story "Camping at Gull Beach." The story contains blanks. Choose the word or words that correctly complete the blanks asked about in Numbers 66 through 68.

Camping at Gull Beach

Ahmad loves to go camping. One of his favorite places to camp is Gull Beach. His family went camping there last summer. His mother packed a tent, food, and supplies. Then Ahmad, his mother, and his father drove to the beach. __(66)__ played games during the drive.

As soon as they arrived, they went swimming in the ocean. Then they set up the tent and cooked dinner. After dinner, they toasted marshmallows over the campfire. Ahmad told ghost stories. The family watched the moon rise over the ocean. Finally, Ahmad __(67)__ keep his eyes open any longer. He went to sleep in his tent.

In the morning, Ahmad's father woke up and made pancakes. After breakfast, Ahmad's family went for a hike. They walked along the beach and saw a lighthouse in the distance.

Next summer, __(68)__ family will go camping again. Ahmad hopes they will return to Gull Beach!

66. Which answer should go in blank (66)?
   A Them
   B Those
   C They

67. Which answer should go in blank (67)?
   F couldnt
   G could'nt
   H couldn't

68. Which answer should go in blank (68)?
   A Ahmads
   B Ahmades
   C Ahmad's

Writing Strategies and Conventions

GO ON

Name _____

Benchmark Assessment • End-of-Year

▶ Read the story "A Day at the Races." The story contains blanks. Choose the word or words that correctly complete the blanks asked about in Numbers 69 through 71.

A Day at the Races

Nina was nervous. Today she would run in her very first race. She woke up and took a shower. Her mother made toast and eggs for breakfast. Then the whole family got into the car to go to the stadium for the race.

At the stadium, Nina made sure her shoes were on tight. __(69)__ were a lot of people waiting for the races to start. Nina found her coaches Miguel and Paul and asked them to wish her good luck. __(70)__ told Nina that she should stretch her legs before the race.

Nina __(71)__ to the starting line. She looked up, but could not see her family. Where were they? The starting bell rang. Nina ran as fast as she could. As she finished the race, she heard her mother call her name. Her family was waiting for her at the finish line!

69. Which answer should go in blank (69)?
   Ⓕ There
   Ⓖ They're
   Ⓗ Their

70. Which answer should go in blank (70)?
   Ⓐ They
   Ⓑ Them
   Ⓒ Their

71. Which answer should go in blank (71)?
   Ⓕ Walks
   Ⓖ is walking
   Ⓗ Walked

Writing Strategies and Conventions

42

GO ON

© Harcourt • Grade 4

Name _____

Benchmark Assessment
End-of-Year

▶ **Read and answer Numbers 72 through 75.**

72. In which sentence below is all **capitalization** correct?

    Ⓐ Every Friday afternoon, Sandra goes swimming at Loon Lake.

    Ⓑ Every Friday Afternoon, Sandra goes swimming at loon lake.

    Ⓒ Every friday afternoon, sandra goes Swimming at Loon Lake.

73. In which sentence below is all **punctuation** correct?

    Ⓕ Harrys desk had a pencil, a ruler and some paper in it.

    Ⓖ Harry's desk had a pencil a ruler and some paper in it.

    Ⓗ Harry's desk had a pencil, a ruler, and some paper in it.

74. In which sentence below is the **suffix** correct?

    Ⓐ My visit to the museum was enjoyment.

    Ⓑ My visit to the museum was enjoyable.

    Ⓒ My visit to the museum was enjoyless.

75. Combine the sentences in the box to make one sentence.

    > Darren kicked the soccer ball.
    > He kicked it into the net.
    > He scored the winning goal.

    Which sentence correctly combines the sentences?

    Ⓕ Darren kicked into the net the soccer ball and he scored the winning goal.

    Ⓖ Darren kicked the soccer ball into the net and scored the winning goal.

    Ⓗ Darren scored the winning goal kicked into the net the soccer ball.

Writing Strategies and Conventions

GO ON

Name _____

For Numbers 76 through 80, read each sentence. Choose the sentence that has the underlined word misspelled. If none of the words are misspelled, choose the answer "No mistake."

76.
- (A) Colorful birds are often found in tropical climates.
- (B) We waited at the station for the train's arrivel.
- (C) How many women were in the swimming class?
- (D) No mistake

77.
- (F) Did you ever look closely at the goose's feathers?
- (G) He gallantly returned the woman's fallen hat.
- (H) All complaints should be given to the main derector.
- (I) No mistake

78.
- (A) You always look radiant in yellow.
- (B) Please spray the disinfectant in the room.
- (C) How much did you have to pay the painist?
- (D) No mistake

79.
- (F) She chose him because he was confident.
- (G) That outfit seems to be a bit outdated.
- (H) We need to call an electrician right away!
- (I) No mistake

80.
- (A) That was an unusually long opera.
- (B) Our tickets are nonrefundable.
- (C) Why did you and he have a disagreement?
- (D) No mistake

Name _____

Benchmark Assessment
End-of-Year

Writing to a Prompt

Everyone has learned how to do new things.
Think about a time when you learned how to do something new.
Now write a story about a time when you learned how to do something new.

Planning Page

▶ Use this space to make your notes before you begin writing. The writing on this page will NOT be scored.

_____
_____
_____
_____
_____
_____
_____
_____
_____
_____
_____
_____
_____

Writing to a Prompt

GO ON

Name _____

**Benchmark Assessment
End-of-Year**

▶ **Begin writing here. The writing on this page and the next WILL be scored.**

Writing to a Prompt

Name _____

**Benchmark Assessment
End-of-Year**

Writing to a Prompt   47

Name _____

Oral Reading Fluency

Benchmark Assessment
End-of-Year

Sometimes ordinary creatures can turn out to be rather unusual. Spiders, for example, can be interesting to study, though we might consider them to be relatively common.

Spiders belong to a group of creatures that have four pairs of legs—eight legs in all. That makes them different from insects, which have three pairs of legs—six legs. This difference is an important way to tell whether a little crawling creature is a spider. The body of a spider has two parts, so if you see only one body part or you see three body parts, you're not looking at a spider.

Spiders have a special skill that is well-known: they produce a fine, very strong silk from glands at the rear of their bodies. This silk has several uses. Probably the one you are most familiar with is the spider web that you might notice on a bush, or in a quiet, unused corner of a room. Spiders also use the silk to line burrows and nests. Spiders also wrap their eggs in the fiber. Finally, spiders make little parachutes with it so they can float through the air to new places.

Observe those spiders crawling and spinning around us every day. They're worth examining!

Dear Thomas,

    You're in for a surprise when you come to visit next month! Do you remember how I always hated to rake the lawn and weed the vegetable garden? Whenever Dad told me to get busy on the jobs, I would tell him that I would do them later. Of course, you also remember that "later" never arrived. Then I would be reminded, and I would find another excuse. The result was always all of us getting "irritated," you might say.

    Anyhow, I was treated to a moral lesson in a BIG way. I delayed doing a school project until the last minute, actually until too late. When I could not complete it on time, I begged my dad to talk to my teacher about an extension of the deadline. Of course, my dad would not do any such thing. He told me he loved me, but that it was very important that I finish my jobs on time. He said that I need *self-discipline*.

    Well, you will find me so full of self-discipline when you get here that I hope you'll still recognize me! I know mowing the lawn and weeding the garden are my jobs, so I just do them. No discussion necessary. Dad and Mom say I've grown up. Of course, I'm proud to help keep the estate's lawn green. See you soon.

                                          Your friend,
                                          Emilio

HARCOURT SCHOOL PUBLISHERS
STORYtown

Grade 4

End-of-Year Assessment

Benchmark Assessments

www.harcourtschool.com

ISBN-13: 978-0-15-358768-9
ISBN-10: 0-15-358768-7

Part No. 9997-87204-5

(Package of 12)